DIABETIC AIR FRYER COOKBOOK

Healthy and Easy Low-Fat, Low-Sugar & Low-Carb
Air-Fryer Recipes for Type 1 & 2 Diabetes with a 42-Day Meal Plan

By Hannah Kingsley

COPYRIGHT DISCLAIMER

© Copyright 2024 - All rights reserved.

The content contained within this book may not be reproduced, duplicated or transmitted without direct written permission from the author or the publisher. Under no circumstances will any blame or legal responsibility be held against the publisher, or author, for any damages, reparation, or monetary loss due to the information contained within this book. Either directly or indirectly.

Legal Notice:

This book is copyright protected. This book is only for personal use. You cannot amend, distribute, sell, use, quote or paraphrase any part, or the content within this book, without the consent of the author or publisher.

Disclaimer Notice:

Please note the information contained within this document is for educational and entertainment purposes only. All effort has been executed to present accurate, up to date, and reliable, complete information. No warranties of any kind are declared or implied. Readers acknowledge that the author is not engaging in the rendering of legal, financial, medical or professional advice. The content within this book has been derived from various sources. Please consult a licensed professional before attempting any techniques outlined in this book. By reading this document, the reader agrees that under no circumstances is the author responsible for any losses, direct or indirect, which are incurred as a result of the use of information contained within this document, including, but not limited to, - errors, omissions, or inaccuracies.

ABOUT THE AUTHOR

BON APPETIT

Hello, dear readers! I'm Hannah Kingsley, the author of the "Diabetic Air-Fryer Cookbook" you're about to explore.

Growing up in the charming countryside of New England, I developed a passion for healthy cooking early on. As a nutritionist and a devoted advocate for diabetic-friendly diets, I've spent years experimenting with wholesome, delicious recipes that cater to those who need to watch their sugar and carb intake.

This cookbook is a culmination of my love for nutritious food and the incredible versatility of the air fryer. I hope these recipes bring joy and health to your kitchen, just as they have to mine.

Table of CONTENTS

-Introduction-   8
An overview of the book and the benefits of air-frying for diabetics

-Chapter 1-   11
GETTING TO KNOW YOUR AIR-FRYER
Basics and essentials of choosing, using, and maintaining an air-fryer for beginners.

-Chapter 2-   14
AIR-FRYING AND YOUR HEALTH
Exploring the health benefits of air-frying and its safety for diabetics.

-Chapter 3-   18
DIABETIC COOKING WITH THE AIR-FRYER
Tips & techniques for diabetic-friendly air-frying and selecting suitable ingredients.

-Chapter 4-   20
BREAKFAST AND BRUNCH DELIGHTS
Healthy, delicious, and easy air-fryer recipes for breakfast and brunch.

Table of CONTENTS

-Chapter 5-   31
LUNCHTIME FAVOURITES
Nutritious and simple air-fryer lunch ideas that keep you full and healthy.

-Chapter 6-   43
DINNER SPECIALS
Satisfying, wholesome, and diabetic-friendly air-fryer dinners to end your day right.

-Chapter 7-   55
SNACKS AND APPETIZERS
Tasty, low-carb snacks and appetizers that are perfect for any time of day.

-Chapter 8-   65
DESSERT SELECTION
Indulgent yet healthy, low-sugar desserts you can make with your air-fryer.

-Chapter 9-   76
MEAL PLANNING
A comprehensive 42-day diabetic meal plan featuring a variety of air-fryer recipes.

-Recipe Index-   79

HANNAH'S WHOLESOME KITCHEN

> "It's not the recipe, but the love and passion of the cook that creates a memorable dish."

Hannah Kingsley

Introduction to Air-Frying for Diabetics

Air-frying has revolutionised the way we prepare meals, especially for those who need to manage their diabetes. This cooking method allows you to enjoy your favourite fried foods with significantly less oil, making it easier to maintain a healthy diet without sacrificing flavour. The air-fryer works by circulating hot air around the food, creating a crispy exterior while keeping the inside tender and moist. It's a perfect tool for preparing meals that are not only delicious but also adhere to the dietary guidelines recommended for diabetics.

In this book, you'll find a variety of recipes that have been carefully crafted to be low in fat, sugar, and carbohydrates, yet full of flavour. Each recipe has been tested to ensure it meets the nutritional needs of those managing diabetes, without compromising on taste or enjoyment.

How to Use This Book

This cookbook is designed to be user-friendly and informative, especially for beginners. Here's a quick guide on how to navigate through it:

- **Chapters Overview:** The book is divided into chapters that cover everything from understanding your air-fryer to detailed meal plans. Start with the introductory chapters if you're new to air-frying.

- **Recipes:** Each recipe section (Breakfast and Brunch, Lunch, Dinner, Snacks and Appetizers, Desserts) provides a variety of options tailored for diabetics. All ingredients and measurements are provided in metric units, ensuring they are suitable and convenient for American readers.
- **Meal Planning:** The meal planning chapter offers a comprehensive 42-day meal plan to help you stay on track with your diet.
- **Index of Recipes:** Use the index at the end of the book to quickly find specific recipes.

Benefits of an Air-Fryer for Diabetics

Air-frying is a fantastic cooking method for those managing diabetes. Here's why:

- **Lower Fat Content:** Air-fryers use significantly less oil compared to traditional frying methods, which helps in reducing calorie intake.
- **Crispy and Delicious:** You can enjoy crispy, tasty foods without the added fats and oils, making it easier to adhere to a low-fat diet.
- **Versatile Cooking:** Air-fryers can bake, roast, grill, and fry, offering a wide range of cooking possibilities.
- **Quick and Convenient:** Cooking times are generally shorter, making it easier to prepare healthy meals quickly.
- **Nutrient Retention:** The rapid cooking process helps retain more nutrients in your food.

I hope this book will be a valuable resource in your journey to healthier eating with the help of your air-fryer.

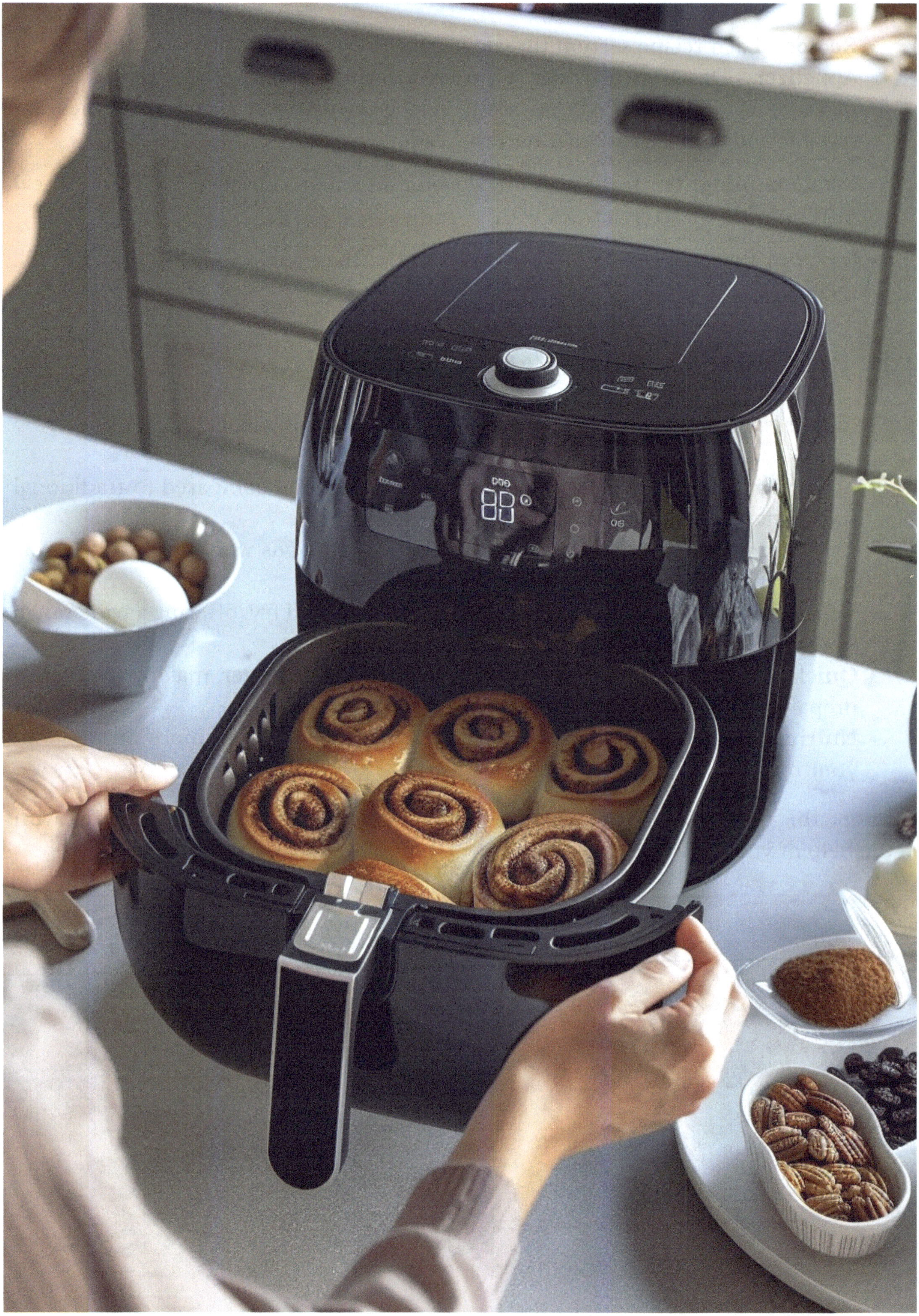

CHAPTER 1:
Getting to Know Your Air-Fryer

What is an Air-Fryer and How Does It Work?

An air-fryer is a modern kitchen appliance designed to cook food by circulating hot air around it. This method mimics the results of deep frying but uses little to no oil, making it a healthier alternative. The air-fryer heats up quickly and uses a fan to distribute the hot air evenly around the food, creating a crispy outer layer while keeping the inside moist and tender.

Main Types of Air-Fryers

There are several types of air-fryers available on the market, each with its own features and benefits. Here are some common types and examples of models available in the United Kingdom:

1. Basket Air-Fryers: These are the most common type and usually come with a pull-out basket where food is placed. Examples include:

- **Philips Airfryer XXL:** Known for its large capacity and powerful performance, suitable for families.
- **Tefal ActiFry Genius XL:** Features a stirring paddle for even cooking without manual intervention.
- **Ninja Air Fryer AF100:** A compact and versatile model with multiple cooking functions.

2. Oven Air-Fryers: These models resemble small convection ovens and often come with multiple racks for cooking different foods simultaneously. Examples include:

- **Ninja Foodi Dual Zone Air Fryer:** Allows you to cook two different foods at the same time with separate controls.
- **Tower T17038 Xpress Pro:** Offers a large capacity and multiple cooking functions including baking and roasting.
- **Instant Vortex Plus Air Fryer Oven:** Features a rotisserie function and various cooking presets.

3. Paddle Air-Fryers: These come with a stirring paddle that automatically stirs the food as it cooks, ensuring even cooking without manual shaking. Examples include:

- Tefal ActiFry Original: Ideal for hands-free cooking with its automatic stirring paddle.

- De'Longhi MultiFry: Combines air frying with a mixing paddle for versatile cooking options.

Choosing the Right Air-Fryer

When selecting an air-fryer, consider the following factors to ensure you choose the best model for your needs:

- **Size and Capacity:** Choose an air-fryer that suits your household size. Smaller models (1-2 litres) are ideal for singles or couples, while larger models (3-5 litres) can accommodate families. For example, the Philips Airfryer XXL is perfect for families, while the Ninja Air Fryer AF100 is better suited for smaller households.

- **Features:** Look for features that will enhance your cooking experience. Important features to consider include:

- *Temperature Control:* Allows you to adjust the cooking temperature to suit different recipes.

- *Timer:* Enables you to set cooking times and avoid overcooking.

- *Pre-set Cooking Programs:* Make cooking easier with pre-set options for common foods like chips, chicken, and fish.

- *Ease of Cleaning:* Consider models with dishwasher-safe parts or easy-to-clean components.

- **Budget:** Air-fryers come in a range of prices. Determine your budget and find a model that offers the best value for money within that range. High-end models like the Philips Airfryer XXL may come with more features, but budget-friendly options like the Tower T17038 Xpress Pro can still provide excellent performance.

- **Additional Considerations:** Think about the noise level of the air-fryer, the warranty provided by the manufacturer, and customer reviews. Reading reviews can provide insights into the reliability and performance of different models.

By carefully considering these factors, you can select an air-fryer that fits your lifestyle and cooking needs, allowing you to enjoy healthier meals, experiment with a variety of recipes, save time in the kitchen, and take full advantage of the convenience and versatility that this innovative appliance offers.

Essential Air-Fryer Accessories

To get the most out of your air-fryer, consider investing in some essential accessories:

- **Baking Pans and Trays:** Useful for baking cakes, muffins, and other desserts.
- **Grill Racks:** Perfect for grilling meats and vegetables.
- **Silicone Mats:** Protect the air-fryer basket and make cleaning easier.
- **Skewers:** Great for making kebabs and skewered foods.
- **Tongs and Spatulas:** Handy tools for turning and serving food.

Cleaning and Maintenance

Proper cleaning and maintenance of your air-fryer are crucial for ensuring its longevity and optimal performance:

- **Regular Cleaning:** Clean the basket and tray after each use with warm, soapy water. Some parts may be dishwasher safe – check the manufacturer's instructions.
- **Deep Cleaning:** Periodically, clean the interior of the air-fryer, including the heating element, to remove any accumulated grease and food particles.
- **Avoid Abrasives:** Use non-abrasive sponges and brushes to avoid damaging the non-stick coating.

CHAPTER 2:
AIR-FRYING AND YOUR HEALTH

Are Air-Fryers Healthy?

Air-fryers have become popular for their ability to produce crispy, delicious food with significantly less oil than traditional frying methods. This reduction in oil can lead to lower calorie intake and fewer unhealthy fats in your diet, which is particularly beneficial for those managing diabetes. By using hot air to cook food, air-fryers help to reduce the formation of harmful compounds that are typically produced during high-temperature cooking methods like deep frying.

Top 5 Health Benefits of Air-Frying

- **Reduced Fat Intake:** Air-frying uses up to 80% less oil than traditional frying, helping you reduce your overall fat consumption. This is crucial for managing weight and blood sugar levels.
- **Lower Calorie Content:** With less oil required, air-fried foods generally have fewer calories, making it easier to maintain a healthy weight and control diabetes.
- **Reduced Risk of Acrylamide Formation:** Acrylamide is a potentially harmful compound formed when starchy foods are fried at high temperatures. Air-frying significantly reduces the production of acrylamide compared to traditional frying.
- **Nutrient Preservation:** The rapid cooking process of an air-fryer helps preserve more nutrients in your food, ensuring you get the maximum health benefits from your meals.
- **Less Grease and Fewer Harmful Fats:** Air-fried foods have less grease and contain fewer trans fats and saturated fats, contributing to better cardiovascular health and improved blood lipid profiles.

Is Air-Frying Safe for Diabetes?

Air-frying is a safe and effective cooking method for those managing diabetes. It allows you to prepare diabetic-friendly meals that are low in fat and calories while still being satisfying and delicious. Here are some reasons why air-frying is a good option for diabetics:

- **Better Blood Sugar Control:** Lower fat intake can improve insulin sensitivity and help manage blood sugar levels more effectively. This can lead to more stable blood glucose levels throughout the day.
- **Weight Management:** Maintaining a healthy weight is essential for managing diabetes, and the reduced calorie content of air-fried foods can support weight loss or maintenance. Achieving and maintaining a healthy weight can significantly improve insulin sensitivity and blood sugar control.
- **Improved Heart Health:** Air-frying helps reduce the intake of unhealthy fats, lowering the risk of cardiovascular disease, which is a common complication of diabetes. Consuming fewer trans fats and saturated fats can lead to better cholesterol levels and overall heart health.
- **Enhanced Nutrient Retention:** The quick cooking process of air-frying helps retain more vitamins and minerals in your food, which is important for overall health and managing diabetes. Nutrient-dense foods can support better metabolic health and improve energy levels.
- **Reduced Oxidative Stress:** Air-frying can lower the formation of harmful compounds that contribute to oxidative stress, a condition linked to various chronic diseases, including diabetes. Reducing oxidative stress can improve overall health and decrease the risk of diabetes-related complications.

By incorporating air-frying into your cooking routine, you can enjoy a variety of tasty meals that align with the dietary recommendations for managing diabetes.

Using Fats and Oils in the Air-Fryer

While air-frying requires significantly less oil than traditional frying methods, the type of oil you use still matters. Here are some tips for using fats and oils in your air-fryer:

- **Choose Healthy Oils:** Opt for oils that are high in healthy fats, such as olive oil, avocado oil, or coconut oil. These oils are better for your heart and overall health.
- **Use Sparingly:** A small amount of oil can go a long way in an air-fryer. Use a spray bottle to lightly coat your food or the air-fryer basket with oil.
- **Avoid Unhealthy Fats:** Stay away from oils high in trans fats or saturated fats, such as vegetable shortening or margarine, as these can negatively impact your health.

By using healthy oils in moderation, you can enhance the flavour and texture of your air-fried foods without compromising your dietary goals.

Air-Fryer Basic Cook Times

To help you get started with your air-fryer, here's a handy chart detailing basic cook times for a variety of diabetic-friendly meats, seafood, and vegetables. All metrics and products are tailored for the American market and follow the guidelines from the the American Diabetes Association.

MEAT & SEAFOOD

Product Name	Prep	Mode	Temperature	Cook Time
Beef Meatballs	5.3 oz	Roast	400°F	12-15 minutes
Beef Sirloin Steak	1 inch thick	Grill	400°F	10-15 minutes
Chicken Breasts	1/2 inch thick	Roast	400°F	15-20 minutes
Chicken Thighs	Bone-in, skin-on	Roast	400°F	25-30 minutes
Cod Loins	3.5 oz each	Bake	350°F	10-12 minutes
Fish Fillets (e.g., cod, haddock)	3.5 oz each	Bake	350°F	10-12 minutes
Lamb Chops	1 inch thick	Roast	400°F	10-12 minutes
Lean Pork Chops	1 inch thick	Roast	400°F	12-15 minutes
Prawns	Shelled and deveined	Grill	350°F	8-10 minutes
Salmon Fillets	1 inch thick	Bake	350°F	10-15 minutes
Tofu	Cubed	Roast	400°F	10-15 minutes
Turkey Breast	Sliced	Bake	350°F	15-20 minutes
Turkey Burgers	3.5 oz each	Grill	400°F	12-15 minutes
White Fish (e.g., sea bass, pollock)	Breaded	Bake	350°F	10-12 minutes

VEGETABLES

Product Name	Prep	Mode	Temperature	Cook Time
Asparagus	Trimmed	Roast	400°F	7-10 minutes
Aubergine	Cubed	Roast	400°F	12-15 minutes
Broccoli	Small florets	Roast	350°F	8-10 minutes
Brussels Sprouts	Halved	Roast	400°F	15-18 minutes
Butternut Squash	Cubed	Bake	400°F	15-20 minutes
Carrots	Sliced 1/4 inch thick	Bake	350°F	15-20 minutes
Cauliflower	Small florets	Roast	350°F	12-15 minutes
Courgettes	Sliced 1/4 inch thick	Roast	350°F	10-12 minutes
Green Beans	Trimmed	Grill	400°F	8-10 minutes
Kale	Lightly oiled	Dehydrate	350°F	4-6 minutes
Mushrooms	Sliced	Roast	350°F	7-10 minutes
Peppers	Cut in half and seeded	Bake	400°F	10-12 minutes
Spinach	Whole leaves, lightly oiled	Dehydrate	350°F	3-5 minutes
Sweet Potatoes	Cut into wedges	Bake	400°F	15-20 minutes
Tomatoes	Halved	Roast	400°F	8-10 minutes

These tables provide a quick reference for preparing a variety of diabetic-friendly foods in your air-fryer, helping you to achieve perfectly cooked meals every time. By understanding these basic cook times and modes, you can confidently experiment with different recipes and enjoy the health benefits of air-frying.

CHAPTER 3:
Diabetic Cooking with the Air-Fryer

Diabetic Air-Fryer Cooking Tips and Techniques

Cooking with an air-fryer helps you prepare delicious, diabetes-friendly meals. Here are essential tips and techniques for best results:

- **Use Minimal Oil:** While air-fryers require much less oil than traditional frying methods, it's still important to use healthy oils like olive oil or avocado oil sparingly.

- **Opt for Whole Foods:** Focus on whole, unprocessed foods such as fresh vegetables, lean meats, and whole grains to create nutrient-dense meals.

- **Avoid High-Sugar Ingredients:** Use natural sweeteners like stevia or monk fruit in place of sugar, and avoid ingredients that are high in refined sugars.

- **Preheat Your Air-Fryer:** Preheating can help ensure that food cooks evenly and achieves a crispy texture.

- **Don't Overcrowd the Basket:** Give your food enough space for air to circulate to ensure even cooking and crispiness.

Should You Air-Fry, Bake, or Grill?

Different cooking methods can impact the nutritional value and taste of your food. Here's a comparison to help you decide which method to use:

- **Air-Frying:** Ideal for achieving a crispy texture with minimal oil, preserving nutrients, and reducing unhealthy fats.

- **Baking:** Good for evenly cooking larger items like casseroles or baked goods, but may require more oil.

- **Grilling:** Adds a smoky flavour and is great for meats and vegetables, but requires outdoor space and can be less convenient.

For diabetics, air-frying is often the best choice as it reduces fat content and calorie intake while retaining the food's nutrients.

Diabetic-Friendly Ingredients for the Air-Fryer

Choosing the right ingredients is crucial for maintaining a diabetic-friendly diet. Here are some key ingredients to consider:

- Lean Proteins: Chicken breast, turkey, fish, tofu, and lean cuts of beef and pork.
- Non-Starchy Vegetables: Broccoli, cauliflower, spinach, kale, peppers, and asparagus.
- Whole Grains: Brown rice, quinoa, and whole-wheat products.
- Healthy Fats: Avocado, nuts, seeds, and olive oil.
- Low-Glycaemic Fruits: Berries, apples, and pears.

These ingredients help manage blood sugar levels and provide essential nutrients without adding unnecessary calories or unhealthy fats.

Adapting Recipes for Low-Sugar and Low-Carb

Adapting your favourite recipes to be low in sugar and carbohydrates can help you manage your diabetes more effectively. Here are some tips:

- Substitute Sweeteners: Use natural sweeteners like stevia or monk fruit instead of sugar.
- Use Low-Carb Flour Alternatives: Replace regular flour with almond flour, coconut flour, or other low-carb options.
- Increase Fibre Content: Add fibre-rich ingredients like flaxseeds, chia seeds, and psyllium husk to your recipes to help control blood sugar levels.
- Reduce Portion Sizes: Serve smaller portions to help control calorie and carbohydrate intake.
- Incorporate More Vegetables: Add extra non-starchy vegetables to your dishes to increase volume and nutrients without adding many calories or carbs.

By making these adjustments, you can enjoy your favourite foods while keeping your blood sugar levels in check.

BREAKFAST AND BRUNCH DELIGHTS

Chapter 4

Avocado & Egg Boats

★★

| 2 servings | 15 minutes |

ingredients

- 2 ripe avocados
- 4 small eggs
- Salt and pepper to taste
- Chopped chives (optional)
- 1 tbsp olive oil

TIP: Ensure the avocados are stable in the air-fryer basket to prevent tipping.

INSTRUCTIONS

1. Preheat the air-fryer to 350°F (Bake mode).
2. Cut the avocados in half and remove the pits.
3. Scoop out some of the flesh to create a larger cavity for the egg.
4. Place the avocado halves in the air-fryer basket and brush with olive oil.
5. Crack an egg into each avocado half.
6. Season with salt and pepper.
7. Cook for 10-12 minutes until the eggs are set.
8. Garnish with chopped chives if desired.

nutrition information
(per serving)

Calories per Serving: 250 kcal
Carbs: 8g   Protein: 10g   Fat: 20g   Sugars: 1g
Cholesterol: 210mg   Sodium: 150mg   Fiber: 7g

SERVINGS
6
muffins

COOKING TIME
15
minutes

DIFFICULTY
★★★
medium

Breakfast Muffins

ingredients

- 3/4 cup whole wheat flour
- 1/2 cup almond flour
- 2 tsp baking powder
- 1/2 tsp baking soda
- 1/4 tsp salt
- 2 large eggs
- 1/2 cup almond milk
- 1/2 cup grated zucchini
- 1/2 cup grated carrot
- 1 tbsp olive oil
- 1 tsp mixed herbs

nutrition information

Calories per muffin: 120 kcal
Carbs: 10g Protein: 4g Fat: 8g Sugars: 2g
Cholesterol: 40mg Sodium: 150mg Fiber: 2g

TIP: These muffins can be stored in an airtight container for up to 3 days.

INSTRUCTIONS

1. Preheat the air-fryer to 320°F (Bake mode).
2. In a bowl, mix the whole wheat flour, almond flour, baking powder, baking soda, and salt.
3. In another bowl, whisk the eggs, almond milk, olive oil, grated zucchini, and grated carrot.
4. Combine the wet and dry ingredients, stirring until just combined.
5. Spoon the batter into silicone muffin cups, filling each about 2/3 full.
6. Place the muffins in the air-fryer basket.
7. Bake for 12-15 minutes until a toothpick inserted into the center comes out clean.
8. Allow to cool on a wire rack before serving.

CINNAMON APPLE SLICES WITH GREEK YOGURT AND NUTS

| 2 servings | 10 minutes | ★☆☆☆☆ |

ingredients

- 2 medium apples
- 1 tsp ground cinnamon
- 1 tsp stevia
- 1 tbsp lemon juice
- 7 oz Greek yogurt
- 2 tbsp walnuts or almonds, chopped

nutrition information

Calories per Serving: 200 kcal
Carbs: 22g **Protein:** 10g **Fat:** 8g **Sugars:** 15g
Cholesterol: 10mg **Sodium:** 40mg **Fiber:** 4g

INSTRUCTIONS

1. Preheat the air-fryer to 350°F (Air Fry mode).
2. Core and slice the apples into thin rings.
3. In a bowl, toss the apple slices with lemon juice, cinnamon, and stevia.
4. Place the apple slices in a single layer in the air-fryer basket.
5. Cook for 8-10 minutes until they are tender and slightly crisp.
6. Divide the Greek yogurt between two bowls or parfait jars.
7. Top each bowl / jar with the warm cinnamon apple slices.
8. Sprinkle with chopped walnuts or almonds.

Spinach and Tomato Breakfast Frittata

🍴 4 servings | 🕐 20 minutes

★★☆☆☆

ingredients

- 6 large eggs
- 1/2 cup skimmed milk
- 3.5 oz fresh spinach, chopped
- 3.5 oz cherry tomatoes, halved
- 1 small onion, finely chopped
- 1.75 oz low-fat feta cheese, crumbled
- Salt and pepper to taste
- 1 tbsp olive oil

nutrition information

Calories per Serving: 160 kcal
Carbs: 4g **Protein:** 12g **Fat:** 10g **Sugars:** 2g
Cholesterol: 210mg **Sodium:** 250mg **Fiber:** 1g

INSTRUCTIONS

1. Preheat the air-fryer to 340°F (Bake mode).
2. In a large bowl, whisk together the eggs and skimmed milk. Season with salt and pepper.
3. Heat olive oil in a pan and sauté the onion until soft.
4. Add the chopped spinach to the pan and cook until wilted.
5. Mix the sautéed spinach and onion into the egg mixture.
6. Pour the mixture into a greased baking dish that fits in your air-fryer basket.
7. Distribute the cherry tomatoes and crumbled feta cheese evenly over the top.
8. Place the dish in the air-fryer and bake for 18-20 minutes until set and golden brown.
9. Let cool slightly before slicing and serving.

SWEET POTATO AND KALE HASH

4 servings | **20 minutes** | ★★★☆☆

ingredients

- 2 large sweet potatoes, peeled and diced
- 3.5 oz fresh kale, stems removed and chopped
- 1 small red bell pepper, diced
- 1 small yellow bell pepper, diced
- 1 small onion, diced
- 2 cloves garlic, minced
- 2 tbsp olive oil
- Salt and pepper to taste
- 4 large eggs

This dish is rich in fiber and provides a balanced breakfast option with protein and healthy fats.

INSTRUCTIONS

1. Preheat the air-fryer to 400°F (Roast mode).
2. In a large bowl, toss the diced sweet potatoes, bell peppers, and onion with 1 tbsp of olive oil. Season with salt and pepper.
3. Place the vegetable mixture in the air-fryer basket and cook for 15 minutes, shaking the basket halfway through.
4. In the last 5 minutes, add the chopped kale to the air-fryer basket and continue to cook until the vegetables are tender and slightly crispy.
5. Meanwhile, in a small pan, heat the remaining 1 tbsp of olive oil and cook the garlic until fragrant.
6. Remove the vegetables from the air-fryer and toss with the cooked garlic.
7. Crack the eggs into the air-fryer basket and cook for 3-5 minutes until the whites are set but the yolks are still runny.
8. Divide the vegetable hash among four plates and top each with a fried egg.

nutrition information

Calories per Serving: 250 kcal
Carbs: 30g **Protein:** 10g **Fat:** 10g **Sugars:** 8g
Cholesterol: 190mg **Sodium:** 150mg **Fiber:** 7g

ingredients

- 1 cup rolled oats
- 1/2 cup almond flour
- 1 tsp baking powder
- 1/2 tsp ground cinnamon
- 1/4 tsp salt
- 1 large egg
- 1/2 cup unsweetened almond milk
- 2 tbsp honey or stevia (adjust based on preference)
- 1/2 cup mixed berries (blueberries, raspberries)
- 1 tsp vanilla extract
- 1 tbsp melted coconut oil

nutrition information

Calories per cup: 120 kcal
Carbs: 15g   Protein: 4g   Fat: 5g   Sugars: 5g
Cholesterol: 25mg   Sodium: 80mg   Fiber: 3g

INSTRUCTIONS

1. Preheat the air-fryer to 320°F (Bake mode).
2. In a large bowl, mix the rolled oats, almond flour, baking powder, ground cinnamon, and salt.
3. In another bowl, whisk the egg, almond milk, honey (or stevia), vanilla extract, and melted coconut oil.
4. Combine the wet and dry ingredients, stirring until just combined.
5. Gently fold in the mixed berries.
6. Spoon the batter into silicone muffin cups, filling each about 2/3 full.
7. Place the muffin cups in the air-fryer basket.
8. Bake for 12-15 minutes until a toothpick inserted into the center comes out clean.
9. Allow to cool on a wire rack before serving.

6 cups | 15 minutes

★★★

BERRY OATMEAL CUPS

MUSHROOM AND SPINACH OMELETTE

🍴 2 servings | 🕐 10 minutes

★★

ingredients

- 4 large eggs
- 3.5 oz fresh spinach, chopped
- 3.5 oz mushrooms, sliced
- 1 small onion, diced
- 1.75 oz grated low-fat cheddar cheese
- 1 tbsp olive oil
- Salt and pepper to taste

nutrition information

Calories per Serving: 200 kcal
Carbs: 4g   Protein: 15g   Fat: 14g   Sugars: 2g
Cholesterol: 250mg   Sodium: 300mg   Fiber: 1g

INSTRUCTIONS

1. Preheat the air-fryer to 350°F (Bake mode).
2. In a pan, heat 1 tbsp of olive oil over medium heat. Sauté the onion and mushrooms until soft.
3. Add the chopped spinach to the pan and cook until wilted. Remove from heat.
4. In a bowl, whisk the eggs and season with salt and pepper.
5. Add the cooked vegetables to the eggs and mix well.
6. Pour the mixture into a greased baking dish that fits in your air-fryer basket.
7. Sprinkle the grated cheddar cheese over the top.
8. Place the dish in the air-fryer and bake for 8-10 minutes until the omelette is set and golden.
9. Let cool slightly before slicing and serving.
10. Serve with a side salad or whole grain toast for a complete meal.

SERVINGS	COOKING TIME	DIFFICULTY
8 bars	15 minutes	★★ easy

Blueberry Almond Breakfast Bars

ingredients

- 1 1/2 cups rolled oats
- 1/2 cup almond flour
- 1 tsp baking powder
- 1/2 tsp ground cinnamon
- 1/4 tsp salt
- 2 large eggs
- 1/2 cup unsweetened almond milk
- 2 tbsp honey or stevia
- 3.5 oz fresh blueberries
- 1.75 oz sliced almonds
- 1 tsp vanilla extract
- 1 tbsp melted coconut oil

INSTRUCTIONS

1. Preheat the air-fryer to 320°F (Bake mode).
2. In a large bowl, mix the rolled oats, almond flour, baking powder, ground cinnamon, and salt.
3. In another bowl, whisk the eggs, almond milk, honey (or stevia), vanilla extract, and melted coconut oil.
4. Combine the wet and dry ingredients, stirring until just combined.
5. Gently fold in the fresh blueberries and sliced almonds.
6. Pour the mixture into a greased baking dish that fits in your air-fryer basket.
7. Bake for 12-15 minutes until a toothpick inserted into the center comes out clean.
8. Allow to cool before cutting into bars and serving.

nutrition information

Calories per bar: 130 kcal
Carbs: 16g Protein: 4g Fat: 6g Sugars: 6g
Cholesterol: 25mg Sodium: 80mg Fiber: 3g

TIP: These breakfast bars can be stored in an airtight container for up to 3 days.

TURKEY SAUSAGE AND VEGGIE BREAKFAST SKILLET

| 4 servings | 20 minutes | ★★★☆☆ |

ingredients

- 7 oz turkey sausage, sliced
- 1 medium sweet potato, peeled and diced
- 1 red bell pepper, diced
- 1 green bell pepper, diced
- 1 small onion, diced
- 2 cloves garlic, minced
- 3.5 oz fresh spinach, chopped
- 2 tbsp olive oil
- Salt and pepper to taste
- Fresh parsley for garnish

INSTRUCTIONS

1. Preheat the air-fryer to 400°F (Roast mode).
2. In a bowl, toss the diced sweet potato, bell peppers, and onion with 1 tbsp olive oil. Season with salt and pepper.
3. Place the vegetable mixture in the air-fryer basket and cook for 10 minutes.
4. Add the sliced turkey sausage to the air-fryer basket and cook for an additional 8 minutes, shaking the basket halfway through.
5. In the last 2 minutes, add the chopped spinach and minced garlic to the air-fryer basket and cook until the spinach is wilted and the vegetables are tender.
6. Transfer the cooked mixture to a serving dish and garnish with fresh parsley before serving.

This hearty breakfast skillet is perfect for a balanced meal, providing protein, healthy fats, and fiber.

nutrition information

Calories per Serving: 220 kcal
Carbs: 18g Protein: 15g Fat: 10g Sugars: 5g
Cholesterol: 55mg Sodium: 500mg Fiber: 4g

Sweet Potato and Black Bean Breakfast Burrito

★★★

| 2 servings | 20 minutes |

ingredients

- 1 large sweet potato, peeled and diced
- 3.5 oz black beans, drained and rinsed
- 1 small red bell pepper, diced
- 1 small onion, finely chopped
- 2 large eggs
- 2 whole wheat tortillas
- 1 tbsp olive oil
- 1.75 oz shredded low-fat cheddar cheese
- 1 avocado, sliced
- Salt and pepper to taste
- Fresh cilantro for garnish

nutrition information
(per serving)

Calories per Serving: 350 kcal
Carbs: 45g Protein: 14g Fat: 14g Sugars: 6g
Cholesterol: 185mg Sodium: 400mg Fiber: 10g

INSTRUCTIONS

1. Preheat the air-fryer to 400°F (Roast mode).
2. In a bowl, toss the diced sweet potato with 1/2 tbsp olive oil, salt, and pepper. Place in the air-fryer basket and roast for 10-12 minutes until tender.
3. In a pan, heat the remaining olive oil over medium heat and sauté the onion and red bell pepper until soft. Add the black beans and cook until heated through. Season with salt and pepper.
4. In a small bowl, whisk the eggs and scramble them in a non-stick pan until just set.
5. Warm the tortillas in the air-fryer for 1-2 minutes until soft and pliable.
6. To assemble, place an equal amount of roasted sweet potato, black bean mixture, scrambled eggs, shredded cheese, and avocado slices on each tortilla.
7. Roll up the tortillas to form burritos and place them seam side down in the air-fryer basket.
8. Air-fry at 350°F (Air Fry mode) for 3-5 minutes until the tortillas are crispy and the cheese is melted.
9. Garnish with fresh cilantro before serving.
10. Serve with a side of salsa or Greek yogurt for added flavor.

LUNCHTIME FAVOURITES
Chapter 5

Lemon Herb Chicken with Roasted Vegetables

★★

🍴 4 servings | 🕐 20 minutes

ingredients

- 4 boneless, skinless chicken breasts
- 2 tbsp olive oil
- 1 lemon, juiced
- 2 cloves garlic, minced
- 1 tsp dried oregano
- 1 tsp dried thyme
- Salt and pepper to taste
- 1 red bell pepper, chopped
- 1 yellow bell pepper, chopped
- 1 zucchini, sliced
- 1 red onion, chopped

nutrition information
(per serving)

Calories per Serving: 300 kcal
Carbs: 10g Protein: 30g Fat: 15g Sugars: 5g
Cholesterol: 80mg Sodium: 250mg Fiber: 3g

INSTRUCTIONS

1. Preheat the air-fryer to 400°F (Air Fry mode).
2. In a bowl, mix the olive oil, lemon juice, minced garlic, dried oregano, dried thyme, salt, and pepper.
3. Place the chicken breasts in the bowl and coat them evenly with the marinade. Let it sit for 10 minutes.
4. Arrange the chopped bell peppers, zucchini, and red onion in the air fryer basket. Drizzle with a bit of olive oil and season with salt and pepper.
5. Place the marinated chicken breasts on top of the vegetables in the air fryer basket.
6. Air fry for 15-20 minutes, turning the chicken halfway through, until the chicken is cooked through and the vegetables are tender.
7. Serve hot, garnished with fresh herbs if desired.

FISH TACOS

4 servings | **15 minutes** | ★★☆☆☆

ingredients

- 4 white fish fillets (such as cod or haddock)
- 1 tbsp olive oil
- 1 tsp paprika
- 1 tsp cumin
- 1/2 tsp garlic powder
- 1/2 tsp salt
- 8 small whole wheat tortillas
- 1 cup shredded cabbage
- 1/2 cup diced tomatoes
- 1/4 cup chopped fresh cilantro
- 1 lime, cut into wedges
- 1/4 cup low-fat Greek yogurt

INSTRUCTIONS

1. Preheat the air-fryer to 400°F (Air Fry mode).
2. In a bowl, mix the olive oil, paprika, cumin, garlic powder, and salt.
3. Coat the fish fillets with the spice mixture.
4. Place the fish fillets in the air fryer basket and cook for 10-12 minutes, turning halfway through, until the fish is cooked through and flaky.
5. Warm the whole wheat tortillas in the air fryer for 1-2 minutes.
6. Assemble the tacos by placing a piece of fish on each tortilla, then topping with shredded cabbage, diced tomatoes, and chopped cilantro.
7. Serve with lime wedges and a dollop of low-fat Greek yogurt.

nutrition information

Calories per Serving: 250 kcal
Carbs: 20g Protein: 22g Fat: 10g Sugars: 3g
Cholesterol: 50mg Sodium: 300mg Fiber: 4g

Stuffed Bell Peppers

🍴 4 servings | 🕐 25 minutes

★★★☆☆

ingredients

- 4 large bell peppers (any color), tops cut off and seeds removed
- 7 oz lean ground turkey
- 1 small onion, finely chopped
- 1 clove garlic, minced
- 1 cup cooked quinoa
- 1 can (14 oz) diced tomatoes, drained
- 1 tsp dried basil
- 1 tsp dried oregano
- Salt and pepper to taste
- 1.75 oz low-fat mozzarella cheese, shredded
- 2 tbsp olive oil

nutrition information

Calories per Serving: 250 kcal
Carbs: 20g **Protein:** 18g **Fat:** 12g **Sugars:** 8g
Cholesterol: 45mg **Sodium:** 300mg **Fiber:** 4g

INSTRUCTIONS

1. Preheat the air-fryer to 350°F (Air Fry mode).
2. In a pan, heat 1 tbsp of olive oil over medium heat. Sauté the onion and garlic until soft.
3. Add the ground turkey to the pan and cook until browned. Season with salt, pepper, dried basil, and dried oregano.
4. Stir in the cooked quinoa and diced tomatoes. Cook for a few more minutes until heated through.
5. Stuff each bell pepper with the turkey and quinoa mixture.
6. Place the stuffed peppers in the air fryer basket and drizzle with the remaining olive oil.
7. Air fry for 20 minutes until the peppers are tender.
8. Sprinkle the shredded mozzarella cheese over the top of the peppers and air fry for an additional 5 minutes until the cheese is melted and bubbly.
9. Serve hot, garnished with fresh herbs if desired.

TURKEY MEATBALLS WITH ZUCCHINI NOODLES

| 4 servings | 20 minutes | ★★★☆☆ |

ingredients

- 14 oz lean ground turkey
- 1 small onion, finely chopped
- 2 cloves garlic, minced
- 1 egg, beaten
- 1/4 cup whole wheat breadcrumbs
- 1/4 cup grated Parmesan cheese
- 1 tsp dried oregano
- 1 tsp dried basil
- Salt and pepper to taste
- 2 large zucchinis, spiralized into noodles
- 2 tbsp olive oil
- 1 cup marinara sauce
- Fresh parsley for garnish

This dish is a low-carb alternative to traditional spaghetti and meatballs, perfect for a healthy lunch.

nutrition information

Calories per Serving: 250 kcal
Carbs: 12g **Protein:** 24g **Fat:** 12g **Sugars:** 6g
Cholesterol: 95mg **Sodium:** 380mg **Fiber:** 3g

INSTRUCTIONS

1. Preheat the air-fryer to 400°F (Air Fry mode).
2. In a bowl, mix the ground turkey, chopped onion, minced garlic, beaten egg, whole wheat breadcrumbs, grated Parmesan cheese, dried oregano, dried basil, salt, and pepper.
3. Form the mixture into small meatballs (about 20).
4. Brush the meatballs with 1 tbsp olive oil and place them in the air fryer basket.
5. Cook for 12-15 minutes, turning halfway through, until the meatballs are cooked through and golden brown.
6. While the meatballs are cooking, heat the remaining olive oil in a pan and sauté the zucchini noodles until just tender.
7. Warm the marinara sauce in a small saucepan.
8. Serve the meatballs over the zucchini noodles, topped with marinara sauce and garnished with fresh parsley.

Stuffed Zucchini Boats with Tuna

🍴 4 servings | 🕐 20 minutes

★★☆☆☆

ingredients

- 4 medium zucchinis, halved lengthwise and seeds scooped out
- 2 cans (5 oz each) tuna in water, drained
- 1 small red onion, finely chopped
- 1/4 cup low-fat Greek yogurt
- 1/4 cup crumbled feta cheese
- 1/4 cup fresh parsley, chopped
- 1/4 cup diced cucumber
- 1 tbsp lemon juice
- Salt and pepper to taste
- 2 tbsp olive oil

nutrition information
Calories per Serving: 180 kcal
Carbs: 8g Protein: 20g Fat: 8g Sugars: 5g
Cholesterol: 35mg Sodium: 290mg Fiber: 2g

INSTRUCTIONS

1. Preheat the air-fryer to 350°F (Air Fry mode).
2. In a large bowl, mix the drained tuna, chopped red onion, Greek yogurt, crumbled feta cheese, chopped parsley, diced cucumber, lemon juice, salt, and pepper until well combined.
3. Stuff each zucchini half with the tuna mixture.
4. Brush the outside of the zucchinis with olive oil.
5. Place the stuffed zucchinis in the air fryer basket in a single layer.
6. Cook for 15-20 minutes, until the zucchinis are tender and the filling is heated through.
7. Serve the stuffed zucchinis warm, garnished with additional fresh parsley if desired.

MEDITERRANEAN VEGGIE WRAPS

| 🍴 4 servings | 🕐 10 minutes | ★ ☆ ☆ ☆ ☆ |

ingredients

- 4 whole wheat tortillas
- 1 red bell pepper, sliced
- 1 yellow bell pepper, sliced
- 1 zucchini, sliced
- 1 red onion, sliced
- 1 tbsp olive oil
- 3.5 oz hummus
- 1.75 oz crumbled feta cheese
- 1 tsp dried oregano
- Salt and pepper to taste
- Fresh spinach leaves

INSTRUCTIONS

1. Preheat the air-fryer to 400°F (Air Fry mode).
2. Toss the sliced bell peppers, zucchini, and red onion with olive oil, dried oregano, salt, and pepper.
3. Place the vegetables in the air fryer basket and cook for 8-10 minutes until tender.
4. Warm the whole wheat tortillas in the air fryer for 1-2 minutes.
5. Spread a layer of hummus on each tortilla.
6. Add a portion of the roasted vegetables on top of the hummus.
7. Sprinkle with crumbled feta cheese and add fresh spinach leaves.
8. Roll up the tortillas and serve warm.

nutrition information

Calories per Serving: 220 kcal
Carbs: 30g **Protein:** 7g **Fat:** 9g **Sugars:** 6g
Cholesterol: 10mg **Sodium:** 300mg **Fiber:** 6g

SERVINGS
4
chicken breasts

COOKING TIME
20 minutes

DIFFICULTY
★★★★
hard

Stuffed Chicken Breasts

ingredients

- 4 boneless, skinless chicken breasts
- 3.5 oz fresh spinach, chopped
- 3.5 oz ricotta cheese
- 1.75 oz sun-dried tomatoes, chopped
- 2 cloves garlic, minced
- 1 tsp dried basil
- 1 tsp dried oregano
- Salt and pepper to taste
- 2 tbsp olive oil

nutrition information

Calories per chicken breast: 320 kcal
Carbs: 5g Protein: 40g Fat: 15g Sugars: 3g
Cholesterol: 100mg Sodium: 250mg Fiber: 2g

Instructions

1. Preheat the air-fryer to 350°F (Bake mode).
2. In a bowl, mix the chopped spinach, ricotta cheese, sun-dried tomatoes, minced garlic, dried basil, dried oregano, salt, and pepper.
3. Carefully slice a pocket into each chicken breast, making sure not to cut all the way through.
4. Stuff each chicken breast with the spinach and ricotta mixture, securing with toothpicks if necessary.
5. Brush the chicken breasts with olive oil and season with salt and pepper.
6. Place the stuffed chicken breasts in the air fryer basket.
7. Bake for 18-20 minutes, turning halfway through, until the chicken is cooked through and golden brown.
8. Remove the toothpicks before serving.

BEEF AND VEGETABLE SKEWERS

4 servings | 15 minutes | ★★★☆☆

ingredients

- 14 oz lean beef, cut into cubes
- 1 red bell pepper, cut into squares
- 1 yellow bell pepper, cut into squares
- 1 red onion, cut into wedges
- 1 zucchini, sliced
- 2 tbsp olive oil
- 2 cloves garlic, minced
- 1 tsp dried rosemary
- 1 tsp dried thyme
- Salt and pepper to taste

nutrition information

Calories per Serving: 250 kcal
Carbs: 10g **Protein:** 25g **Fat:** 12g **Sugars:** 5g
Cholesterol: 70mg **Sodium:** 200mg **Fiber:** 3g

INSTRUCTIONS

1. Preheat the air-fryer to 400°F (Grill mode).
2. In a bowl, mix the olive oil, minced garlic, dried rosemary, dried thyme, salt, and pepper.
3. Toss the beef cubes and vegetables in the marinade until well coated.
4. Thread the beef and vegetables alternately onto the skewers.
5. Place the skewers in the air fryer basket.
6. Grill for 12-15 minutes, turning occasionally, until the beef is cooked to your desired doneness and the vegetables are tender.
7. Serve hot, garnished with fresh herbs if desired.

Mustard Salmon

★★★

| 🍴 4 servings | 🕐 15 minutes |

ingredients

- 4 salmon fillets
- 2 tbsp Dijon mustard
- 2 tbsp honey
- 1 tsp olive oil
- 1 tsp lemon juice
- Salt and pepper to taste
- Fresh dill for garnish

Serve with a side of steamed vegetables or a green salad for a complete meal.

INSTRUCTIONS

1. Preheat the air-fryer to 400°F (Air Fry mode).
2. In a small bowl, mix the Dijon mustard, honey, olive oil, lemon juice, salt, and pepper.
3. Brush the honey mustard mixture over the salmon fillets.
4. Place the salmon fillets in the air fryer basket.
5. Air-fry for 10-12 minutes until the salmon is cooked through and has a golden glaze.
6. Garnish with fresh dill before serving.

nutrition information
(per serving)

Calories per Serving: 290 kcal
Carbs: 8g **Protein:** 26g **Fat:** 16g **Sugars:** 7g
Cholesterol: 70mg **Sodium:** 250mg **Fiber:** 0g

STUFFED EGGPLANT WITH QUINOA AND SPINACH

4 servings | 30 minutes

★★★★☆

ingredients

- 2 large eggplants, halved lengthwise
- 1 cup cooked quinoa
- 7 oz fresh spinach, chopped
- 1 small onion, finely chopped
- 2 cloves garlic, minced
- 1 can (14 oz) diced tomatoes, drained
- 1.75 oz feta cheese, crumbled
- 2 tbsp olive oil
- 1 tsp dried oregano
- 1 tsp dried basil
- Salt and pepper to taste
- Fresh parsley for garnish

nutrition information
Calories per serving: 320 kcal
Carbs: 35g Protein: 10g Fat: 18g Sugars: 10g
Cholesterol: 20mg Sodium: 300mg Fiber: 8g

INSTRUCTIONS

1. Preheat the air-fryer to 400°F (Air Fry mode).
2. Scoop out the flesh of the eggplants, leaving a 1cm thick shell. Chop the scooped-out flesh and set aside.
3. Brush the eggplant shells with olive oil, season with salt and pepper, and place them in the air fryer basket. Cook for 10 minutes until slightly tender.
4. In a pan, heat 1 tbsp of olive oil over medium heat. Sauté the chopped onion and garlic until soft.
5. Add the chopped eggplant flesh, spinach, and drained diced tomatoes to the pan. Cook until the spinach is wilted and the mixture is heated through.
6. Stir in the cooked quinoa, dried oregano, dried basil, salt, and pepper. Mix well.
7. Stuff the eggplant shells with the quinoa and vegetable mixture.
8. Place the stuffed eggplants back in the air fryer basket and cook for an additional 15 minutes until the eggplants are tender and the filling is golden brown.
9. Sprinkle the crumbled feta cheese over the stuffed eggplants and cook for another 5 minutes.
10. Garnish with fresh parsley before serving.

ingredients

- 1 can (14 oz) chickpeas, drained and rinsed
- 1 small carrot, grated
- 1 small zucchini, grated
- 1 small onion, finely chopped
- 2 cloves garlic, minced
- 1/4 cup whole wheat breadcrumbs
- 1 tbsp ground flaxseed
- 1 tsp cumin
- 1 tsp paprika
- Salt and pepper to taste
- 2 tbsp olive oil

nutrition information
Calories per serving: 200 kcal
Carbs: 25g Protein: 7g Fat: 8g Sugars: 3g
Cholesterol: 0mg Sodium: 250mg Fiber: 6g

INSTRUCTIONS

1. Preheat the air-fryer to 350°F (Air Fry mode).
2. In a food processor, blend the chickpeas until smooth.
3. Transfer the blended chickpeas to a bowl and add the grated carrot, grated zucchini, chopped onion, minced garlic, whole wheat breadcrumbs, ground flaxseed, cumin, paprika, salt, and pepper.
4. Mix well until all ingredients are combined.
5. Form the mixture into 8 small patties.
6. Brush the patties with olive oil on both sides.
7. Place the patties in the air fryer basket and cook for 12-15 minutes, flipping halfway through, until golden brown and crispy.
8. Serve the patties with a side salad or whole grain pita bread.

4 servings | 15 minutes

★★★

CHICKPEA VEGETABLE PATTIES

DINNER SPECIALS
Chapter 6

Herb-Crusted Cod with Asparagus

★★

| 4 servings | 15 minutes |

ingredients

- 4 cod fillets
- 2 tbsp olive oil
- 2 cloves garlic, minced
- 1 tbsp fresh parsley, chopped
- 1 tbsp fresh dill, chopped
- 1 lemon, zested and juiced
- Salt and pepper to taste
- 1 bunch asparagus, trimmed

nutrition information
(per serving)

Calories per Serving: 290 kcal
Carbs: 4g Protein: 28g Fat: 18g Sugars: 2g
Cholesterol: 70mg Sodium: 250mg Fiber: 2g

INSTRUCTIONS

1. Preheat the air-fryer to 400°F (Air Fry mode).
2. In a small bowl, mix the olive oil, minced garlic, chopped parsley, chopped dill, lemon zest, lemon juice, salt, and pepper.
3. Brush the cod fillets with the herb mixture.
4. Place the cod fillets in the air fryer basket and cook for 10-12 minutes, until the cod is cooked through and flakes easily with a fork.
5. While the cod is cooking, toss the asparagus with a little olive oil, salt, and pepper.
6. Add the asparagus to the air fryer basket during the last 5 minutes of cooking.
7. Serve the cod fillets with the roasted asparagus, garnished with extra fresh herbs and lemon wedges.

TANDOORI CAULIFLOWER STEAKS WITH CHICKEN TIKKA

4 servings | **25 minutes** | ★★★☆☆

ingredients

Tandoori Cauliflower Steaks:
- 1 large cauliflower, cut into 1-inch thick steaks
- 1 cup plain Greek yogurt (low-fat)
- 1 tbsp olive oil
- 2 cloves garlic, minced
- 1 tbsp grated fresh ginger
- 1 tsp ground turmeric, cumin, coriander, paprika, garam masale (each)
- Juice of 1 lemon
- Salt and pepper to taste
- Fresh cilantro for garnish

Chicken Tikka:
- 14 oz boneless, skinless chicken thighs, cut into bite-sized pieces
- 1 cup plain Greek yogurt (low-fat)
- 2 tbsp lemon juice
- 1 tbsp grated fresh ginger
- 2 cloves garlic, minced
- 1 tsp ground cumin, coriander, paprika, garam masala (each)
- 1/2 tsp ground turmeric, cayenne pepper
- Salt and pepper to taste

INSTRUCTIONS

1. Preheat the air-fryer to 400°F (Air Fry mode).
2. For the cauliflower steaks, in a large bowl, mix the Greek yogurt, olive oil, minced garlic, grated ginger, ground turmeric, ground cumin, ground coriander, paprika, garam masala, lemon juice, salt, and pepper. Coat the cauliflower steaks with the tandoori marinade, ensuring they are evenly covered.
3. For the chicken tikka, in another bowl, mix the Greek yogurt, lemon juice, grated ginger, minced garlic, ground cumin, ground coriander, paprika, garam masala, ground turmeric, cayenne pepper (if using), salt, and pepper. Add the chicken pieces and coat them evenly with the marinade.
4. Place the cauliflower steaks in the air fryer basket in a single layer and cook for 15-20 minutes, flipping halfway through, until the cauliflower is tender and slightly charred. Remove and set aside.
5. Add the marinated chicken pieces to the air fryer basket and cook for 10-12 minutes, until the chicken is cooked through and slightly charred.
6. Serve the tandoori cauliflower steaks with the chicken tikka, garnished with fresh cilantro.

nutrition information

Calories per serving: 320 kcal
Carbs: 15g Protein: 30g Fat: 14g Sugars: 7g
Cholesterol: 80mg Sodium: 400mg Fiber: 5g

Beef and Broccoli Stir-Fry

4 servings | 20 minutes

★★★★☆

ingredients

- 14 oz lean beef, thinly sliced
- 2 cups broccoli florets
- 1 red bell pepper, sliced
- 2 tbsp soy sauce (low sodium)
- 1 tbsp hoisin sauce (low sugar)
- 1 tbsp sesame oil
- 2 cloves garlic, minced
- 1 tsp grated fresh ginger
- 1 tsp cornstarch
- 1 tbsp water
- 1 tbsp olive oil
- Sesame seeds for garnish
- Fresh green onions for garnish

nutrition information

Calories per Serving: 280 kcal
Carbs: 10g   Protein: 30g   Fat: 12g   Sugars: 4g
Cholesterol: 70mg   Sodium: 500mg   Fiber: 4g

INSTRUCTIONS

1. Preheat the air-fryer to 400°F (Air Fry mode).
2. In a bowl, mix the soy sauce, hoisin sauce, sesame oil, minced garlic, grated ginger, cornstarch, and water to create the marinade.
3. Add the sliced beef to the marinade and let it sit for 10 minutes.
4. Toss the broccoli florets and sliced red bell pepper with olive oil, salt, and pepper.
5. Place the marinated beef in the air fryer basket and cook for 10 minutes.
6. Add the broccoli and red bell pepper to the air fryer basket with the beef and continue to air-fry for another 10 minutes, or until the beef is cooked through and the vegetables are tender.
7. Serve the beef and broccoli stir-fry garnished with sesame seeds and fresh green onions.

PESTO-CRUSTED PORK CHOPS WITH ROASTED CHERRY TOMATOES

4 servings | 20 minutes | ★★★☆☆

ingredients

- 4 boneless pork chops
- 1/2 cup basil pesto (store-bought or homemade)
- 1/4 cup grated Parmesan cheese
- 2 cups cherry tomatoes
- 1 tbsp olive oil
- Salt and pepper to taste
- Fresh basil leaves for garnish

nutrition information

Calories per Serving: 350 kcal
Carbs: 6g Protein: 30g Fat: 22g Sugars: 3g
Cholesterol: 85mg Sodium: 350mg Fiber: 2g

INSTRUCTIONS

1. Preheat the air-fryer to 400°F (Air Fry mode).
2. Spread a thin layer of basil pesto over each pork chop, then sprinkle with grated Parmesan cheese.
3. Place the pork chops in the air fryer basket and cook for 15-18 minutes, until the pork is cooked through and the tops are golden brown.
4. Toss the cherry tomatoes with olive oil, salt, and pepper.
5. Add the cherry tomatoes to the air fryer basket during the last 5 minutes of cooking.
6. Serve the pesto-crusted pork chops with the roasted cherry tomatoes, garnished with fresh basil leaves.

ingredients

- 2 large eggplants, sliced into 1/2-inch thick rounds
- 1 cup whole wheat breadcrumbs
- 1/2 cup grated Parmesan cheese
- 2 large eggs, beaten
- 1 cup marinara sauce (low sugar)
- 1 cup shredded mozzarella cheese (low-fat)
- 1 tsp dried oregano
- 1 tsp dried basil
- Salt and pepper to taste
- Fresh basil leaves for garnish

nutrition information

Calories per serving: 350 kcal
Carbs: 30g Protein: 15g Fat: 18g Sugars: 10g
Cholesterol: 100mg Sodium: 500mg Fiber: 8g

INSTRUCTIONS

1. Preheat the air-fryer to 400°F (Air Fry mode).
2. Set up a breading station with two bowls: one with beaten eggs and one with a mixture of whole wheat breadcrumbs, grated Parmesan cheese, dried oregano, dried basil, salt, and pepper.
3. Dip each eggplant slice in the beaten eggs, then coat with the breadcrumb mixture.
4. Place the breaded eggplant slices in the air fryer basket in a single layer and cook for 10 minutes, flipping halfway through, until golden brown and crispy.
5. In a baking dish that fits your air fryer, layer the cooked eggplant slices with marinara sauce and shredded mozzarella cheese.
6. Air-fry for an additional 10-15 minutes until the cheese is melted and bubbly.
7. Serve the eggplant Parmesan garnished with fresh basil leaves.

4 servings | 25 minutes

★★★

EGGPLANT PARMESAN

HADDOCK FISH CAKES WITH TARTAR SAUCE

4 servings | 20 minutes | ★★★☆☆

ingredients

Fish Cakes:
- 14 oz haddock fillets, cooked and flaked
- 2 medium potatoes, peeled, boiled, and mashed
- 1 small onion, finely chopped
- 2 tbsp fresh parsley, chopped
- 1 egg, beaten
- 1 tsp Dijon mustard
- Salt and pepper to taste
- 1/2 cup whole wheat breadcrumbs
- 1 tbsp olive oil

Tartar Sauce:
- 1/2 cup plain Greek yogurt
- 2 tbsp capers, chopped
- 2 gherkins, finely chopped
- 1 tbsp lemon juice
- 1 tsp Dijon mustard
- Salt and pepper to taste

INSTRUCTIONS

1. Preheat the air-fryer to 400°F (Air Fry mode).
2. In a large bowl, mix the flaked haddock, mashed potatoes, chopped onion, fresh parsley, beaten egg, Dijon mustard, salt, and pepper until well combined.
3. Form the mixture into small patties and coat them with whole wheat breadcrumbs.
4. Brush the fish cakes with olive oil and place them in the air fryer basket.
5. Cook for 10-12 minutes, flipping halfway through, until the fish cakes are golden brown and crispy.
6. While the fish cakes are cooking, prepare the tartar sauce by mixing the Greek yogurt, chopped capers, finely chopped gherkins, lemon juice, Dijon mustard, salt, and pepper in a bowl.
7. Serve the fish cakes with tartar sauce on the side.

nutrition information

Calories per serving: 320 kcal
Carbs: 25g **Protein:** 25g **Fat:** 12g **Sugars:** 5g
Cholesterol: 75mg **Sodium:** 450mg **Fiber:** 4g

Coconut Shrimp with Mango Salsa

★★★

4 servings | 15 minutes

ingredients

- Ingredients for Coconut Shrimp:
- 14 oz large shrimp, peeled and deveined
- 1/2 cup coconut flour
- 2 large eggs, beaten
- 1 cup unsweetened shredded coconut
- 1/2 cup panko breadcrumbs
- 1/2 tsp salt
- 1/2 tsp black pepper
- Ingredients for Mango Salsa:
- 1 ripe mango, diced
- 1/2 red bell pepper, diced
- 1/4 red onion, finely chopped
- 1/4 cup fresh cilantro, chopped
- Juice of 1 lime
- Salt and pepper to taste

INSTRUCTIONS

1. Preheat the air-fryer to 400°F (Air Fry mode).
2. Set up a breading station with three bowls: one with coconut flour, one with beaten eggs, and one with a mixture of shredded coconut, panko breadcrumbs, salt, and pepper.
3. Dredge each shrimp in coconut flour, dip in beaten eggs, and coat with the coconut breadcrumb mixture.
4. Place the breaded shrimp in the air fryer basket in a single layer and cook for 10-12 minutes, until golden brown and crispy.
5. While the shrimp is cooking, prepare the mango salsa by combining diced mango, red bell pepper, red onion, cilantro, lime juice, salt, and pepper in a bowl.
6. Serve the coconut shrimp with mango salsa on the side.

nutrition information
(per serving)

Calories per Serving: 300 kcal
Carbs: 20g   Protein: 25g   Fat: 12g   Sugars: 10g
Cholesterol: 180mg   Sodium: 600mg   Fiber: 5g

LEMON GARLIC SCALLOPS WITH ROASTED BRUSSELS SPROUTS

4 servings | **20 minutes** | ★★☆☆☆

ingredients

- 17.5 oz large scallops, cleaned
- 3 tbsp olive oil
- 3 cloves garlic, minced
- Zest and juice of 1 lemon
- 1 tsp dried oregano
- Fresh parsley for garnish
- Lemon wedges for serving
- 17.5 oz Brussels sprouts, trimmed and halved
- 1 tsp garlic powder
- Salt and pepper to taste

nutrition information
Calories per Serving: 260 kcal
Carbs: 12g **Protein:** 26g **Fat:** 14g **Sugars:** 2g
Cholesterol: 40mg **Sodium:** 350mg **Fiber:** 5g

INSTRUCTIONS

1. Preheat the air-fryer to 400°F (Air Fry mode).
2. In a large bowl, mix the olive oil, minced garlic, lemon zest, lemon juice, dried oregano, salt, and pepper.
3. Add the scallops to the bowl and toss to coat them evenly with the lemon garlic mixture.
4. Place the scallops in the air fryer basket in a single layer and cook for 8-10 minutes, shaking the basket halfway through, until the scallops are opaque and cooked through. Remove and set aside.
5. In a separate bowl, toss the trimmed and halved Brussels sprouts with olive oil, garlic powder, salt, pepper, and lemon zest.
6. Place the Brussels sprouts in the air fryer basket and cook for 12-15 minutes, shaking the basket halfway through, until they are tender and slightly crispy.
7. Serve the lemon garlic scallops with the roasted Brussels sprouts, garnished with fresh parsley and lemon wedges.

Lamb Shawarma with Roasted Vegetables

🍴 4 servings | 🕐 25 minutes

★★★☆☆

ingredients

- 17.5 oz lamb fillets, cut into strips
- 1 tbsp olive oil
- 2 cloves garlic, minced
- 1 tsp ground cumin, coriander, paprika (each)
- 1/2 tsp ground turmeric, cinnamon, allspice (each)
- Salt and pepper to taste
- 1 large red onion, sliced
- 1 large red bell pepper, sliced
- 1 large yellow bell pepper, sliced
- 1 cup cherry tomatoes, halved
- Fresh parsley for garnish
- Lemon wedges for serving

nutrition information

Calories per Serving: 380 kcal
Carbs: 12g Protein: 30g Fat: 22g Sugars: 6g
Cholesterol: 100mg Sodium: 400mg Fiber: 4g

INSTRUCTIONS

1. Preheat the air-fryer to 400°F (Air Fry mode).
2. In a large bowl, mix the olive oil, minced garlic, ground cumin, ground coriander, ground paprika, ground turmeric, ground cinnamon, ground allspice, salt, and pepper.
3. Add the lamb strips to the bowl and coat them evenly with the spice mixture.
4. In a separate bowl, toss the sliced red onion, red bell pepper, yellow bell pepper, and cherry tomatoes with a little olive oil, salt, and pepper.
5. Place the lamb strips in the air fryer basket and cook for 15 minutes, shaking the basket halfway through.
6. Add the vegetables to the air fryer basket with the lamb and cook for an additional 10 minutes until the lamb is cooked through and the vegetables are tender.
7. Serve the lamb shawarma with the roasted vegetables, garnished with fresh parsley and lemon wedges.

FALAFEL WITH TZATZIKI SAUCE

4 servings | 15 minutes | ★★★★☆

ingredients

Falafel:
- 1 can (14 oz) chickpeas, drained and rinsed
- 1 small onion, finely chopped
- 2 cloves garlic, minced
- 1/4 cup fresh parsley, chopped
- 1/4 cup fresh cilantro, chopped
- 1 tsp ground cumin
- 1 tsp ground coriander
- 1/2 tsp baking powder
- 3 tbsp whole wheat flour
- Salt and pepper to taste
- 2 tbsp olive oil

Tzatziki Sauce:
- 1 cup plain Greek yogurt (low-fat)
- 1/2 cucumber, grated and drained
- 1 clove garlic, minced
- 1 tbsp lemon juice
- 1 tbsp fresh dill, chopped
- Salt and pepper to taste

INSTRUCTIONS

1. Preheat the air-fryer to 350°F (Air Fry mode).
2. In a food processor, combine the chickpeas, onion, garlic, parsley, cilantro, ground cumin, ground coriander, baking powder, whole wheat flour, salt, and pepper. Pulse until well combined but still slightly chunky.
3. Form the mixture into small balls or patties, about 1 inch in diameter.
4. Brush the falafel balls with olive oil and place them in the air fryer basket.
5. Air-fry for 12-15 minutes, turning halfway through, until the falafel is golden brown and crispy.
6. While the falafel is cooking, prepare the tzatziki sauce by combining the Greek yogurt, grated cucumber, minced garlic, lemon juice, chopped dill, salt, and pepper in a bowl. Mix well.
7. Serve the falafel with the tzatziki sauce on the side.

nutrition information

Calories per serving: 280 kcal
Carbs: 30g **Protein:** 10g **Fat:** 12g **Sugars:** 5g
Cholesterol: 5mg **Sodium:** 400mg **Fiber:** 8g

SERVINGS
4
servings

COOKING TIME
30
minutes

DIFFICULTY
★★★
medium

BBQ Chicken Drumsticks with Sweet Potato Wedges

ingredients

- 8 chicken drumsticks
- 2 large sweet potatoes, cut into wedges
- 3 tbsp BBQ sauce (sugar-free or low-sugar)
- 2 tbsp olive oil
- 1 tsp smoked paprika
- 1 tsp garlic powder
- 1 tsp onion powder
- Salt and pepper to taste
- Fresh parsley for garnish

nutrition information

Calories per serving: 350 kcal
Carbs: 25g Protein: 28g Fat: 15g Sugars: 8g
Cholesterol: 90mg Sodium: 420mg Fiber: 5g

INSTRUCTIONS

1. Preheat the air-fryer to 400°F (Air Fry mode).
2. In a large bowl, toss the chicken drumsticks with 2 tablespoons of BBQ sauce, smoked paprika, garlic powder, onion powder, salt, and pepper. Ensure the drumsticks are evenly coated.
3. In another bowl, toss the sweet potato wedges with olive oil, salt, and pepper.
4. Place the chicken drumsticks in the air fryer basket and cook for 15 minutes.
5. After 15 minutes, add the sweet potato wedges to the air fryer basket with the chicken drumsticks.
6. Continue to air-fry for another 15 minutes, or until the chicken is cooked through and the sweet potato wedges are tender and crispy.
7. Brush the remaining BBQ sauce over the chicken drumsticks and air-fry for an additional 2-3 minutes to caramelize the sauce.
8. Serve the BBQ chicken drumsticks with sweet potato wedges, garnished with fresh parsley.

Snacks and Appetizers

Chapter 7

Spinach and Feta Stuffed Mushrooms

🍴 4 servings | 🕐 15 minutes

★★☆☆☆

ingredients

- 8 large portobello mushrooms
- 3.5 oz fresh spinach, chopped
- 3.5 oz feta cheese, crumbled
- 1 small onion, finely chopped
- 2 cloves garlic, minced
- 2 tbsp olive oil
- Salt and pepper to taste

nutrition information

Calories per Serving: 180 kcal
Carbs: 6g Protein: 7g Fat: 14g Sugars: 3g
Cholesterol: 20mg Sodium: 320mg Fiber: 2g

INSTRUCTIONS

1. Preheat the air-fryer to 350°F (Air Fry mode).
2. Clean the mushrooms and remove the stems. Brush the mushroom caps with olive oil and season with salt and pepper.
3. In a pan, heat 1 tbsp of olive oil over medium heat. Sauté the onion and garlic until soft and fragrant.
4. Add the chopped spinach to the pan and cook until wilted. Remove from heat and stir in the crumbled feta cheese.
5. Stuff each mushroom cap with the spinach and feta mixture.
6. Place the stuffed mushrooms in the air-fryer basket.
7. Air-fry for 12-15 minutes until the mushrooms are tender and the filling is golden brown.
8. Serve warm.

SWEET POTATO CHIPS

- 4 servings
- 20 minutes
- ★☆☆☆☆

ingredients

- 2 large sweet potatoes, thinly sliced
- 1 tbsp olive oil
- 1 tsp paprika
- 1/2 tsp garlic powder
- Salt and pepper to taste
- Fresh rosemary for garnish (optional)

nutrition information

Calories per Serving: 130 kcal
Carbs: 20g   Protein: 2g   Fat: 5g   Sugars: 5g
Cholesterol: 0mg   Sodium: 150mg   Fiber: 4g

INSTRUCTIONS

1. Preheat the air-fryer to 400°F (Air Fry mode).
2. In a large bowl, toss the thinly sliced sweet potatoes with olive oil, paprika, garlic powder, salt, and pepper until evenly coated.
3. Place the sweet potato slices in the air fryer basket in a single layer. You may need to cook in batches depending on the size of your air fryer.
4. Cook for 15-20 minutes, shaking the basket halfway through, until the sweet potato chips are crispy and golden brown.
5. Serve garnished with fresh rosemary if desired.

Prosciutto-Wrapped Asparagus

⭐

| 4 servings | 10 minutes |

ingredients

- 12 asparagus stalks, trimmed
- 6 slices prosciutto, halved lengthwise
- 1 tbsp olive oil
- 1/2 tsp black pepper
- Fresh lemon wedges for serving
- Fresh herbs for garnish (optional)

INSTRUCTIONS

1. Preheat the air-fryer to 400°F (Air Fry mode).
2. Wrap each asparagus stalk with a half slice of prosciutto.
3. Brush the wrapped asparagus with olive oil and sprinkle with black pepper.
4. Place the prosciutto-wrapped asparagus in the air fryer basket in a single layer.
5. Cook for 8-10 minutes until the prosciutto is crispy and the asparagus is tender.
6. Serve with fresh lemon wedges and garnish with fresh herbs if desired.

nutrition information
(per serving)

Calories per Serving: 90 kcal
Carbs: 2g Protein: 6g Fat: 6g Sugars: 1g
Cholesterol: 10mg Sodium: 400mg Fiber: 1g

VEGGIE SKEWERS

4 servings | **15 minutes** | ★☆☆☆☆

ingredients

- 12 cherry tomatoes
- 1 yellow bell pepper, cut into chunks
- 1 red bell pepper, cut into chunks
- 1 cucumber, sliced into thick rounds
- 12 small mozzarella balls
- 2 tbsp olive oil
- 1 tsp Italian seasoning
- Salt and pepper to taste
- Fresh basil leaves for garnish
- Balsamic glaze for serving (optional)

nutrition information

Calories per Serving: 120 kcal
Carbs: 6g **Protein:** 5g **Fat:** 9g **Sugars:** 3g
Cholesterol: 15mg **Sodium:** 150mg **Fiber:** 2g

INSTRUCTIONS

1. Preheat the air-fryer to 350°F (Air Fry mode).
2. Thread cherry tomatoes, bell pepper chunks, cucumber slices, and mozzarella balls onto skewers.
3. Brush the skewers with olive oil and sprinkle with Italian seasoning, salt, and pepper.
4. Place the veggie skewers in the air fryer basket in a single layer.
5. Cook for 10-12 minutes, turning halfway through, until the vegetables are tender and slightly charred.
6. Serve the veggie skewers garnished with fresh basil leaves and a drizzle of balsamic glaze if desired.

SERVINGS	COOKING TIME	DIFFICULTY
4 servings	10 minutes	★★ easy

Stuffed Mini Bell Peppers

ingredients

- 12 mini bell peppers, halved and seeds removed
- 1/2 cup low-fat cream cheese
- 1/4 cup crumbled goat cheese
- 1/4 cup finely chopped fresh herbs (parsley, chives, and dill)
- 1 clove garlic, minced
- Salt and pepper to taste
- 1 tbsp olive oil

nutrition information
Calories per serving: 120 kcal
Carbs: 6g   Protein: 5g   Fat: 9g   Sugars: 4g
Cholesterol: 20mg   Sodium: 150mg   Fiber: 2g

INSTRUCTIONS

1. Preheat the air-fryer to 350°F (Air Fry mode).
2. In a bowl, mix the low-fat cream cheese, crumbled goat cheese, finely chopped fresh herbs, minced garlic, salt, and pepper until well combined.
3. Stuff each mini bell pepper half with the cheese mixture.
4. Brush the outsides of the stuffed mini bell peppers with olive oil.
5. Place the stuffed mini bell peppers in the air fryer basket in a single layer.
6. Cook for 8-10 minutes, until the peppers are tender and the cheese filling is golden brown.
7. Serve warm, garnished with additional fresh herbs if desired.

ZUCCHINI FRIES

4 servings | **15 minutes** | ★☆☆☆☆

ingredients

- 2 medium zucchinis, cut into fries
- 1/2 cup whole wheat breadcrumbs
- 1/4 cup grated Parmesan cheese
- 1 tsp Italian seasoning
- 1/2 tsp garlic powder
- 1/2 tsp onion powder
- Salt and pepper to taste
- 1 egg, beaten
- 1 tbsp olive oil

nutrition information

Calories per Serving: 130 kcal
Carbs: 12g Protein: 5g Fat: 7g Sugars: 3g
Cholesterol: 45mg Sodium: 250mg Fiber: 2g

INSTRUCTIONS

1. Preheat the air-fryer to 400°F (Air Fry mode).
2. In a shallow bowl, mix the whole wheat breadcrumbs, grated Parmesan cheese, Italian seasoning, garlic powder, onion powder, salt, and pepper.
3. Dip each zucchini fry into the beaten egg, then coat with the breadcrumb mixture.
4. Place the coated zucchini fries in the air fryer basket in a single layer.
5. Cook for 12-15 minutes, shaking the basket halfway through, until the zucchini fries are crispy and golden brown.
6. Serve the zucchini fries warm with your favorite dipping sauce.

ingredients

- 1 can (14 oz) chickpeas, drained and rinsed
- 1 tbsp olive oil
- 1 tsp smoked paprika
- 1/2 tsp garlic powder
- 1/2 tsp ground cumin
- 1/4 tsp cayenne pepper (optional)
- Salt and pepper to taste

nutrition information
Calories per serving: 150 kcal
Carbs: 18g Protein: 5g Fat: 7g Sugars: 2g
Cholesterol: 0mg Sodium: 220mg Fiber: 5g

INSTRUCTIONS

1. Preheat the air-fryer to 400°F (Air Fry mode).
2. In a bowl, toss the drained and rinsed chickpeas with olive oil, smoked paprika, garlic powder, ground cumin, cayenne pepper (if using), salt, and pepper until evenly coated.
3. Place the chickpeas in the air fryer basket in a single layer.
4. Cook for 12-15 minutes, shaking the basket halfway through, until the chickpeas are crispy and golden brown.
5. Serve warm or at room temperature as a crunchy and healthy snack.

4 servings | 15 minutes

CRISPY CHICKPEAS

PARMESAN GARLIC GREEN BEANS

4 servings | 10 minutes | ★☆☆☆☆

ingredients

- 14 oz fresh green beans, trimmed
- 2 tbsp olive oil
- 1/4 cup grated Parmesan cheese
- 2 cloves garlic, minced
- 1 tsp Italian seasoning
- Salt and pepper to taste
- Lemon wedges for serving

nutrition information

Calories per Serving: 120 kcal
Carbs: 8g **Protein:** 4g **Fat:** 9g **Sugars:** 3g
Cholesterol: 5mg **Sodium:** 200mg **Fiber:** 4g

INSTRUCTIONS

1. Preheat the air-fryer to 400°F (Air Fry mode).
2. In a large bowl, toss the green beans with olive oil, grated Parmesan cheese, minced garlic, Italian seasoning, salt, and pepper until well coated.
3. Place the green beans in the air fryer basket in a single layer.
4. Cook for 8-10 minutes, shaking the basket halfway through, until the green beans are tender and slightly crispy.
5. Serve the Parmesan garlic green beans with lemon wedges on the side.

Baked Avocado Fries

★★

4 servings | 10 minutes

ingredients

- 2 ripe avocados, sliced into wedges
- 1/2 cup whole wheat breadcrumbs
- 1/4 cup grated Parmesan cheese
- 1 tsp smoked paprika
- 1/2 tsp garlic powder
- 1/2 tsp onion powder
- Salt and pepper to taste
- 1 egg, beaten
- Olive oil spray

nutrition information
(per serving)

Calories per Serving: 220 kcal
Carbs: 12g   Protein: 5g   Fat: 18g   Sugars: 1g
Cholesterol: 45mg   Sodium: 150mg   Fiber: 7g

INSTRUCTIONS

1. Preheat the air-fryer to 400°F (Air Fry mode).
2. In a shallow bowl, mix the whole wheat breadcrumbs, grated Parmesan cheese, smoked paprika, garlic powder, onion powder, salt, and pepper.
3. Dip each avocado wedge into the beaten egg, then coat with the breadcrumb mixture.
4. Place the coated avocado wedges in the air fryer basket in a single layer and spray lightly with olive oil.
5. Cook for 8-10 minutes, shaking the basket halfway through, until the avocado fries are crispy and golden brown.
6. Serve the avocado fries warm with your favorite dipping sauce.

DESSERT SELECTION
Chapter 8

Berry Crisp

★★

| 🍴 4 servings | 🕐 20 minutes |

ingredients

- 2 cups mixed berries (strawberries, blueberries, raspberries, blackberries)
- 1 tbsp lemon juice
- 2 tbsp sugar substitute (such as erythritol)
- 1/2 cup almond flour
- 1/4 cup rolled oats
- 1/4 cup chopped nuts (almonds or walnuts)
- 1/4 cup melted coconut oil
- 1 tsp ground cinnamon

nutrition information
(per serving)

Calories per Serving: 180 kcal
Carbs: 16g   Protein: 4g   Fat: 12g   Sugars: 7g
Cholesterol: 0mg   Sodium: 5mg   Fiber: 6g

INSTRUCTIONS

1. Preheat the air-fryer to 350°F (Bake mode).
2. In a bowl, mix the berries with lemon juice and 1 tbsp of the sugar substitute. Divide the berry mixture into four small, air-fryer safe ramekins.
3. In another bowl, combine the almond flour, rolled oats, chopped nuts, melted coconut oil, cinnamon, and the remaining 1 tbsp of sugar substitute. Mix until crumbly.
4. Sprinkle the crumble mixture evenly over the berries in each ramekin.
5. Place the ramekins in the air fryer basket and cook for 15-20 minutes, until the topping is golden brown and the berries are bubbly.
6. Serve warm, optionally with a dollop of Greek yogurt or a drizzle of sugar-free syrup.

CINNAMON ROLL BITES

🍴 12 bites | 🕐 10 minutes | ★★☆☆☆

ingredients

- 3.5 oz whole wheat flour
- 1.75 oz almond flour
- 1 tsp baking powder
- 1/4 tsp salt
- 2 tbsp stevia
- 1 large egg
- 3.5 tbsp unsweetened almond milk
- 1 tsp vanilla extract
- 1 tbsp melted coconut oil

Cinnamon Filling:
- 2 tbsp melted coconut oil
- 2 tbsp ground cinnamon
- 1 tbsp stevia

Glaze:
- 2 tbsp Greek yogurt
- 1 tbsp stevia
- 1/2 tsp vanilla extract

INSTRUCTIONS

1. Preheat the air-fryer to 350°F (Bake mode).
2. In a bowl, mix the whole wheat flour, almond flour, baking powder, salt, and stevia.
3. In another bowl, whisk the egg, almond milk, vanilla extract, and melted coconut oil.
4. Combine the wet and dry ingredients, stirring until a dough forms.
5. Roll out the dough on a floured surface into a rectangle about 1/4 inch thick.
6. Brush the dough with melted coconut oil and sprinkle evenly with the cinnamon and stevia mixture.
7. Roll the dough tightly into a log and cut into 12 equal pieces.
8. Place the cinnamon roll bites in the air-fryer basket.
9. Bake for 8-10 minutes until golden brown.
10. While the bites are baking, mix the Greek yogurt, stevia, and vanilla extract to make the glaze.
11. Drizzle the glaze over the warm cinnamon roll bites before serving.

nutrition information

Calories per bite: 70 kcal
Carbs: 8g **Protein:** 2g **Fat:** 3g **Sugars:** 2g
Cholesterol: 15mg **Sodium:** 70mg **Fiber:** 1g

SERVINGS	COOKING TIME	DIFFICULTY
6 mini cheesecakes	15 minutes	★★★ medium

Mini Cheesecakes

ingredients

For the crust:
- 1/2 cup almond flour
- 2 tbsp melted butter
- 1 tbsp sugar substitute (such as erythritol)

For the filling:
- 8 oz cream cheese, softened
- 1/4 cup Greek yogurt
- 1/4 cup sugar substitute (such as erythritol)
- 1 large egg
- 1 tsp vanilla extract
- 1 tbsp lemon juice

INSTRUCTIONS

1. Preheat the air-fryer to 320°F (Bake mode).
2. In a bowl, combine the almond flour, melted butter, and sugar substitute until the mixture resembles wet sand.
3. Divide the mixture evenly among 6 silicone muffin cups, pressing it down firmly to form the crust.
4. In another bowl, beat the cream cheese until smooth. Add the Greek yogurt, sugar substitute, egg, vanilla extract, and lemon juice, and mix until well combined.
5. Pour the cheesecake filling over the crusts in the muffin cups, filling each about 3/4 full.
6. Place the muffin cups in the air fryer basket and cook for 12-15 minutes, until the cheesecakes are set but still slightly jiggly in the center.
7. Allow the mini cheesecakes to cool to room temperature, then refrigerate for at least 2 hours before serving.
8. Optionally, top with fresh berries or a dollop of sugar-free whipped cream before serving.

nutrition information

Calories per serving: 180 kcal
Carbs: 6g   Protein: 5g   Fat: 16g   Sugars: 2g
Cholesterol: 60mg   Sodium: 150mg   Fiber: 1g

CINNAMON APPLE RINGS

4 servings | 10 minutes | ★☆☆☆☆

ingredients

- 2 large apples (Granny Smith or Fuji), cored and sliced into rings
- 1 tbsp melted coconut oil
- 1 tsp ground cinnamon
- 1 tbsp sugar substitute (such as erythritol)
- 1/4 cup almond flour

nutrition information

Calories per Serving: 80 kcal
Carbs: 14g **Protein:** 1g **Fat:** 3g **Sugars:** 8g
Cholesterol: 0mg **Sodium:** 0mg **Fiber:** 3g

INSTRUCTIONS

1. Preheat the air-fryer to 350°F (Bake mode).
2. In a bowl, combine the melted coconut oil, ground cinnamon, sugar substitute, and almond flour.
3. Dip each apple ring into the mixture, coating both sides evenly.
4. Place the coated apple rings in the air fryer basket in a single layer.
5. Cook for 8-10 minutes, flipping halfway through, until the apple rings are tender and golden brown.
6. Serve warm, optionally with a dollop of Greek yogurt or a sprinkle of extra cinnamon.

ingredients

- 2 ripe bananas, mashed
- 1 cup rolled oats
- 1/4 cup almond butter
- 1/4 cup sugar substitute (such as erythritol)
- 1 tsp vanilla extract
- 1/2 tsp ground cinnamon
- 1/4 cup dark chocolate chips (sugar-free)

nutrition information

Calories per cookie: 90 kcal
Carbs: 12g **Protein:** 2g **Fat:** 4g **Sugars:** 3g
Cholesterol: 0mg **Sodium:** 20mg **Fiber:** 2g

INSTRUCTIONS

1. Preheat the air-fryer to 350°F (Bake mode).
2. In a large bowl, combine the mashed bananas, rolled oats, almond butter, sugar substitute, vanilla extract, and ground cinnamon until well mixed.
3. Fold in the dark chocolate chips.
4. Drop spoonfuls of the cookie dough onto parchment paper, shaping them into cookies.
5. Place the parchment paper with the cookies in the air fryer basket.
6. Cook for 10-12 minutes, until the cookies are golden brown and set.
7. Let the cookies cool on a wire rack before serving.

12 cookies | 10 minutes

★★

BANANA OAT COOKIES

CHOCOLATE AVOCADO BROWNIES

- 9 brownies | 15 minutes | ★★★☆☆

ingredients

- 1 ripe avocado, mashed
- 1/2 cup sugar substitute (such as erythritol)
- 2 large eggs
- 1 tsp vanilla extract
- 1/2 cup almond flour
- 1/4 cup unsweetened cocoa powder
- 1/2 tsp baking powder
- 1/4 tsp salt
- 1/4 cup dark chocolate chips (sugar-free)

nutrition information

Calories per Serving: 120 kcal
Carbs: 10g Protein: 4g Fat: 8g Sugars: 1g
Cholesterol: 40mg Sodium: 80mg Fiber: 3g

INSTRUCTIONS

1. Preheat the air-fryer to 320°F (Bake mode).
2. In a bowl, mix the mashed avocado and sugar substitute until smooth.
3. Add the eggs and vanilla extract, and mix until well combined.
4. In another bowl, combine the almond flour, cocoa powder, baking powder, and salt.
5. Gradually add the dry ingredients to the wet ingredients, mixing until a smooth batter forms.
6. Fold in the dark chocolate chips.
7. Pour the batter into a greased 8-inch square pan that fits into your air fryer.
8. Cook in the air fryer for 12-15 minutes, until a toothpick inserted in the center comes out clean.
9. Allow the brownies to cool before cutting into squares and serving.

Baked Pears with Cinnamon and Walnuts

★

| 4 servings | 15 minutes |

ingredients

- 2 large pears, halved and cored
- 1/4 cup chopped walnuts
- 2 tbsp sugar substitute (such as erythritol)
- 1 tsp ground cinnamon
- 1 tbsp melted butter
- Greek yogurt or low-fat whipped cream for serving (optional)

INSTRUCTIONS

1. Preheat the air-fryer to 350°F (Bake mode).
2. In a small bowl, mix the chopped walnuts, sugar substitute, ground cinnamon, and melted butter.
3. Place the pear halves in the air fryer basket, cut side up.
4. Spoon the walnut mixture into the center of each pear half.
5. Cook in the air fryer for 12-15 minutes, until the pears are tender and the topping is golden brown.
6. Serve warm, optionally with a dollop of Greek yogurt or low-fat whipped cream.

nutrition information
(per serving)

Calories per Serving: 140 kcal
Carbs: 18g   Protein: 2g   Fat: 8g   Sugars: 10g
Cholesterol: 5mg   Sodium: 0mg   Fiber: 4g

LEMON BLUEBERRY SCONES

🍴 8 scones | 🕐 12 minutes | ★★★☆☆

ingredients

- 1 1/2 cups almond flour
- 1/4 cup coconut flour
- 1/4 cup sugar substitute (such as erythritol)
- 1 tsp baking powder
- 1/4 tsp salt
- 1/4 cup cold butter, cubed
- 2 large eggs
- 1/4 cup unsweetened almond milk
- 1 tsp vanilla extract
- Zest of 1 lemon
- 1/2 cup fresh blueberries

nutrition information

Calories per Serving: 170 kcal
Carbs: 10g Protein: 6g Fat: 13g Sugars: 2g
Cholesterol: 50mg Sodium: 150mg Fiber: 4g

INSTRUCTIONS

1. Preheat the air-fryer to 350°F (Bake mode).
2. In a large bowl, combine the almond flour, coconut flour, sugar substitute, baking powder, and salt.
3. Cut in the cold butter using a pastry cutter or fork until the mixture resembles coarse crumbs.
4. In another bowl, whisk together the eggs, almond milk, vanilla extract, and lemon zest.
5. Add the wet ingredients to the dry ingredients and mix until just combined.
6. Gently fold in the blueberries.
7. Scoop the dough into 8 equal portions and shape into small scones. Place them on a piece of parchment paper in the air fryer basket.
8. Cook for 10-12 minutes, until the scones are golden brown and set.
9. Allow the scones to cool slightly before serving.

Raspberry Almond Tart

🍴 8 slices | 🕐 25 minutes

★★★★☆

ingredients

For the crust:
- 1 cup almond flour
- 2 tbsp coconut flour
- 2 tbsp melted butter
- 2 tbsp sugar substitute (such as erythritol)
- 1 egg white

For the filling:
- 1/2 cup almond flour
- 1/4 cup unsweetened almond milk
- 1/4 cup sugar substitute (such as erythritol)
- 2 large eggs
- 1 tsp almond extract
- 1 cup fresh raspberries

nutrition information
Calories per Serving: 160 kcal
Carbs: 8g **Protein:** 6g **Fat:** 13g **Sugars:** 3g
Cholesterol: 45mg **Sodium:** 35mg **Fiber:** 4g

INSTRUCTIONS

1. Preheat the air-fryer to 320°F (Bake mode).
2. In a bowl, mix the almond flour, coconut flour, melted butter, sugar substitute, and egg white until well combined. Press the mixture evenly into the bottom of a greased tart pan that fits into your air fryer.
3. Place the tart pan in the air fryer and bake for 8-10 minutes, until the crust is golden brown. Remove from the air fryer and let it cool slightly.
4. In another bowl, whisk together the almond flour, almond milk, sugar substitute, eggs, and almond extract until smooth.
5. Pour the filling over the cooled crust and smooth the top.
6. Arrange the fresh raspberries on top of the filling.
7. Place the tart pan back in the air fryer and bake for 15-18 minutes, until the filling is set and golden around the edges.
8. Allow the tart to cool to room temperature before slicing and serving.

CHOCOLATE ZUCCHINI BREAD

10 slices | 25 minutes | ★★★★☆

ingredients

- 1 cup almond flour
- 1/4 cup coconut flour
- 1/4 cup unsweetened cocoa powder
- 1/2 cup sugar substitute (such as erythritol)
- 1 tsp baking powder
- 1/2 tsp baking soda
- 1/4 tsp salt
- 2 large eggs
- 1/4 cup melted coconut oil
- 1 tsp vanilla extract
- 1 cup grated zucchini (excess moisture squeezed out)
- 1/2 cup dark chocolate chips (sugar-free)

nutrition information

Calories per Serving: 140 kcal
Carbs: 10g **Protein:** 4g **Fat:** 10g **Sugars:** 2g
Cholesterol: 35mg **Sodium:** 100mg **Fiber:** 4g

INSTRUCTIONS

1. Preheat the air-fryer to 320°F (Bake mode).
2. In a large bowl, combine the almond flour, coconut flour, cocoa powder, sugar substitute, baking powder, baking soda, and salt.
3. In another bowl, whisk together the eggs, melted coconut oil, and vanilla extract.
4. Add the wet ingredients to the dry ingredients and mix until just combined.
5. Fold in the grated zucchini and dark chocolate chips.
6. Pour the batter into a greased loaf pan that fits into your air fryer.
7. Place the loaf pan in the air fryer and bake for 20-25 minutes, until a toothpick inserted into the center comes out clean.
8. Allow the bread to cool in the pan for 10 minutes, then transfer to a wire rack to cool completely before slicing and serving.

CHAPTER 9: MEAL PLANNING

Welcome to the Meal Planning Chapter!
Managing diabetes can be challenging, but with careful meal planning and healthy, delicious recipes, you can maintain stable blood sugar levels and enjoy a varied and satisfying diet. This chapter provides a comprehensive 42-day meal plan featuring a range of air-fryer recipes that are specifically designed to be diabetes-friendly.

Why Meal Planning is Important
Meal planning is a crucial aspect of managing diabetes. It helps you control your carbohydrate intake, maintain a balanced diet, and avoid unhealthy food choices. By planning your meals in advance, you can ensure that you are consuming the right nutrients in the correct portions, which is essential for blood sugar control and overall health.

How to Use This Meal Plan
This 42-day meal plan is designed to provide balanced nutrition while keeping your blood sugar levels stable. Each day includes breakfast, lunch, dinner, snacks, and a dessert, all prepared using your air fryer. The recipes are easy to follow and use ingredients that are readily available in your local store.

Customizing Your Meal Plan
While this meal plan offers a structured approach to healthy eating, it is also flexible. Feel free to swap meals or adjust portion sizes according to your preferences and nutritional needs. Always consult with your healthcare provider or a registered dietitian before making significant changes to your diet, especially if you have specific dietary restrictions or health concerns.

Final Thoughts
I hope this meal plan inspires you to embrace healthy eating and enjoy the benefits of using an air fryer. By incorporating these recipes into your daily routine, you can take control of your diabetes management while still enjoying delicious and satisfying meals.

Now, let's dive into the 42-day meal plan and start your journey to healthier eating!

42-DAY DIABETIC MEAL PLAN

DAY	BREAKFAST	LUNCH	DINNER	SNACK	DESSERT
Week 1					
1	Air-Fryer Avocado & Egg Boats	Lemon Herb Chicken with Roasted Vegetables	Herb-Crusted Cod with Asparagus	Crispy Chickpeas	Berry Crisp
2	Breakfast Muffins	Fish Tacos	Stuffed Bell Peppers	Sweet Potato Chips	Chocolate Avocado Brownies
3	Cinnamon Apple Slices with Greek Yogurt and Nuts	Turkey Meatballs with Zucchini Noodles	Tandoori Cauliflower Steaks with Chicken Tikka	Prosciutto-Wrapped Asparagus	Lemon Blueberry Scones
4	Spinach and Tomato Breakfast Frittata	Stuffed Zucchini Boats with Tuna	Beef and Broccoli Stir-Fry	Parmesan Garlic Green Beans	Mini Cheesecakes
5	Sweet Potato and Kale Hash	Mediterranean Veggie Wraps	Mustard Salmon	Zucchini Fries	Raspberry Almond Tart
6	Berry Oatmeal Cups	Stuffed Chicken Breasts	Coconut Shrimp with Mango Salsa	Veggie Skewers	Cinnamon Roll Bites
7	Mushroom and Spinach Omelette	Beef and Vegetable Skewers	Pesto-Crusted Pork Chops with Roasted Cherry Tomatoes	Stuffed Mini Bell Peppers	Baked Pears with Cinnamon and Walnuts
Week 2					
8	Blueberry Almond Breakfast Bars	Haddock Fish Cakes with Tartar Sauce	Lamb Shawarma with Roasted Vegetables	Baked Avocado Fries	Chocolate Zucchini Bread
9	Turkey Sausage and Veggie Breakfast Skillet	Lemon Herb Chicken with Roasted Vegetables	Eggplant Parmesan	Crispy Chickpeas	Cinnamon Apple Rings
10	Sweet Potato and Black Bean Breakfast Burrito	Stuffed Zucchini Boats with Tuna	Mustard Salmon	Sweet Potato Chips	Banana Oat Cookies
11	Air-Fryer Avocado & Egg Boats	Fish Tacos	Lemon Garlic Scallops with Roasted Brussels Sprouts	Parmesan Garlic Green Beans	Lemon Blueberry Scones
12	Breakfast Muffins	Turkey Meatballs with Zucchini Noodles	Beef and Broccoli Stir-Fry	Zucchini Fries	Berry Crisp
13	Cinnamon Apple Slices with Greek Yogurt and Nuts	Mediterranean Veggie Wrap	Pesto-Crusted Pork Chops with Roasted Cherry Tomatoes	Sweet Potato Chips	Chocolate Avocado Brownies
14	Spinach and Tomato Breakfast Frittata	Stuffed Bell Peppers	Lamb Shawarma with Roasted Vegetables	Veggie Skewers	Mini Cheesecakes
Week 3					
15	Sweet Potato and Kale Hash	Lemon Herb Chicken with Roasted Vegetables	Tandoori Cauliflower Steaks with Chicken Tikka	Prosciutto-Wrapped Asparagus	Raspberry Almond Tart
16	Berry Oatmeal Cups	Beef and Vegetable Skewers	Mustard Salmon	Parmesan Garlic Green Beans	Cinnamon Roll Bites
17	Mushroom and Spinach Omelette	Haddock Fish Cakes with Tartar Sauce	Stuffed Chicken Breasts	Zucchini Fries	Baked Pears with Cinnamon and Walnuts
18	Blueberry Almond Breakfast Bars	Fish Tacos	Coconut Shrimp with Mango Salsa	Stuffed Mini Bell Peppers	Chocolate Zucchini Bread
19	Turkey Sausage and Veggie Breakfast Skillet	Stuffed Zucchini Boats with Tuna	Eggplant Parmesan	Crispy Chickpeas	Cinnamon Apple Rings
20	Sweet Potato and Black Bean Breakfast Burrito	Mediterranean Veggie Wraps	Lamb Shawarma with Roasted Vegetables	Sweet Potato Chips	Banana Oat Cookies
21	Air-Fryer Avocado & Egg Boats	Lemon Herb Chicken with Roasted Vegetables	Beef and Broccoli Stir-Fry	Parmesan Garlic Green Beans	Lemon Blueberry Scones

42-DAY DIABETIC MEAL PLAN

DAY	BREAKFAST	LUNCH	DINNER	SNACK	DESSERT
Week 4					
22	Breakfast Muffins	Turkey Meatballs with Zucchini Noodles	Mustard Salmon	Zucchini Fries	Berry Crisp
23	Cinnamon Apple Slices with Greek Yogurt and Nuts	Fish Tacos	Lemon Garlic Scallops with Roasted Brussels Sprouts	Prosciutto-Wrapped Asparagus	Chocolate Avocado Brownies
24	Spinach and Tomato Breakfast Frittata	Haddock Fish Cakes with Tartar Sauce	Pesto-Crusted Pork Chops with Roasted Cherry Tomatoes	Veggie Skewers	Mini Cheesecakes
25	Sweet Potato and Kale Hash	Stuffed Bell Peppers	Coconut Shrimp with Mango Salsa	Stuffed Mini Bell Peppers	Raspberry Almond Tart
26	Berry Oatmeal Cups	Mediterranean Veggie Wraps	Tandoori Cauliflower Steaks with Chicken Tikka	Zucchini Fries	Cinnamon Roll Bites
27	Mushroom and Spinach Omelette	Lemon Herb Chicken with Roasted Vegetables	Beef and Vegetable Skewers	Parmesan Garlic Green Beans	Baked Pears with Cinnamon and Walnuts
28	Blueberry Almond Breakfast Bars	Fish Tacos	Eggplant Parmesan	Sweet Potato Chips	Chocolate Zucchini Bread
Week 5					
29	Turkey Sausage and Veggie Breakfast Skillet	Stuffed Bell Peppers	Lamb Shawarma with Roasted Vegetables	Crispy Chickpeas	Cinnamon Apple Rings
30	Sweet Potato and Black Bean Breakfast Burrito	Haddock Fish Cakes with Tartar Sauce	Mustard Salmon	Prosciutto-Wrapped Asparagus	Banana Oat Cookies
31	Air-Fryer Avocado & Egg Boats	Lemon Herb Chicken with Roasted Vegetables	Stuffed Chicken Breasts	Zucchini Fries	Lemon Blueberry Scones
32	Breakfast Muffins	Fish Tacos	Beef and Broccoli Stir-Fry	Veggie Skewers	Berry Crisp
33	Cinnamon Apple Slices with Greek Yogurt and Nuts	Turkey Meatballs with Zucchini Noodles	Pesto-Crusted Pork Chops with Roasted Cherry Tomatoes	Sweet Potato Chips	Chocolate Avocado Brownies
34	Spinach and Tomato Breakfast Frittata	Stuffed Bell Peppers	Coconut Shrimp with Mango Salsa	Stuffed Mini Bell Peppers	Mini Cheesecakes
35	Sweet Potato and Kale Hash	Mediterranean Veggie Wraps	Lemon Garlic Scallops with Roasted Brussels	Zucchini Fries	Raspberry Almond Tart
Week 6					
36	Berry Oatmeal Cups	Lemon Herb Chicken with Roasted Vegetables	Tandoori Cauliflower Steaks with Chicken Tikka	Parmesan Garlic Green Beans	Cinnamon Roll Bites
37	Mushroom and Spinach Omelette	Fish Tacos	Lamb Shawarma with Roasted Vegetables	Prosciutto-Wrapped Asparagus	Baked Pears with Cinnamon and Walnuts
38	Blueberry Almond Breakfast Bars	Haddock Fish Cakes with Tartar Sauce	Beef and Vegetable Skewers	Sweet Potato Chips	Chocolate Zucchini Bread
39	Turkey Sausage and Veggie Breakfast Skillet	Lemon Herb Chicken with Roasted Vegetables	Mustard Salmon	Crispy Chickpeas	Cinnamon Apple Rings
40	Sweet Potato and Black Bean Breakfast Burrito	Turkey Meatballs with Zucchini Noodles	Eggplant Parmesan	Veggie Skewers	Banana Oat Cookies
41	Air-Fryer Avocado & Egg Boats	Fish Tacos	Coconut Shrimp with Mango Salsa	Stuffed Mini Bell Peppers	Lemon Blueberry Scones
42	Breakfast Muffins	Mediterranean Veggie Wraps	Beef and Broccoli Stir-Fry	Zucchini Fries	Berry Crisp

RECIPE INDEX

Avocado & Egg Boats	21
Baked Avocado Fries	64
Baked Pears with Cinnamon and Walnuts	72
Banana Oat Cookies	70
BBQ Chicken Drumsticks with Sweet Potato Wedges	54
Beef and Broccoli Stir-Fry	46
Beef and Vegetable Skewers	39
Berry Crisp	66
Berry Oatmeal Cups	26
Blueberry Almond Breakfast Bars	28
Breakfast Muffins	22
Chickpea Vegetable Patties	42
Chocolate Avocado Brownies	71
Chocolate Zucchini Bread	75
Cinnamon Apple Rings	69
Cinnamon Apple Slices with Greek Yogurt and Nuts	23
Cinnamon Roll Bites	67
Coconut Shrimp with Mango Salsa	50
Crispy Chickpeas	62
Eggplant Parmesan	48
Falafel with Tzatziki Sauce	53
Fish Tacos	33
Haddock Fish Cakes with Tartar Sauce	49
Herb-Crusted Cod with Asparagus	44
Lamb Shawarma with Roasted Vegetables	52
Lemon Blueberry Scones	73
Lemon Garlic Scallops with Roasted Brussels Sprouts	51
Lemon Herb Chicken with Roasted Vegetables	32
Mediterranean Veggie Wraps	37
Mini Cheesecakes	68
Mushroom and Spinach Omelette	27
Mustard Salmon	40
Parmesan Garlic Green Beans	63
Pesto-Crusted Pork Chops with Roasted Cherry Tomatoes	47
Prosciutto-Wrapped Asparagus	58
Raspberry Almond Tart	74
Spinach and Feta Stuffed Mushrooms	56
Spinach and Tomato Breakfast Frittata	24
Stuffed Bell Peppers	34
Stuffed Chicken Breasts	38
Stuffed Eggplant with Quinoa and Spinach	41
Stuffed Mini Bell Peppers	60
Stuffed Zucchini Boats with Tuna	36
Sweet Potato and Black Bean Breakfast Burrito	30
Sweet Potato and Kale Hash	25
Sweet Potato Chips	57
Tandoori Cauliflower Steaks with Chicken Tikka	45
Turkey Meatballs with Zucchini Noodles	35
Turkey Sausage and Veggie Breakfast Skillet	29
Veggie Skewers	59
Zucchini Fries	61

Made in United States
Orlando, FL
09 December 2024